Teacher by Day

Praise for *Teacher by Day*

With wellness-centered logic, experience-rooted humor, impeccable clarity, and step-by-step instructions, *Teacher by Day* is a powerfully timely handbook that will help educators keep their passion for imparting knowledge while maintaining their sanity in an ever more demanding profession. It should be a go-to resource for anyone in education. I'm not even a teacher, but this book made me want to be!

—**Nic Stone**, *New York Times* bestselling author of *Dear Martin*

What makes this book different is that Yvette doesn't just write about balance and boundaries, she embodies them. She talks the talk and walks the walk, which is why *Teacher by Day* feels so authentic and inspiring. Reading it reminded me that thriving as an educator and in life is not only possible, it is essential, and this book makes the journey feel empowering every step of the way.

—**Da'Nall Wilmer**, educator, author, and mentor

Teachers give everything—time, energy, and heart—yet are too often left depleted. In *Teacher by Day*, Dr. Yvette Dixon Ledford offers a candid, uplifting guide to teacher well-being. Through sharp analogies, unforgettable stories, catchy sayings, and real TLC, she reveals how educators can protect their health, reclaim their worth, and reignite their purpose. Her reflections on being "out here working for food" challenge readers to rethink the value of their labor during the prime of their lives. This essential book is both a mirror and a roadmap for teachers ready to thrive, not just survive.

—**Dr. Natalie Odom Pough**, university professor, teacher, and recipient of the Presidential Award for Excellence in Mathematics and Science

DR. YVETTE DIXON LEDFORD

Teacher by DAY

A NO-GUILT GUIDE

to BOUNDARIES,

BALANCE, *and* BLISS

This book is available at special discounts when purchased in quantity for educational purposes or for use as premiums, promotions, or fundraisers. For inquiries and details, contact the publisher at books@daveburgessconsulting.com.

Published by Dave Burgess Consulting, Inc.
Vancouver, WA
DaveBurgessConsulting.com

Library of Congress Control Number: 2026935049
Paperback ISBN: 978-1-968898-17-5
Ebook ISBN: 978-1-968898-18-2

Cover and interior design by Liz Schreiter
Edited and produced by Reading List Editorial
ReadingListEditorial.com

To my incredible parents, Charlie and Gwendolyn Dixon—thank you for instilling in me a deep love of learning and the belief that education has the power to transform lives. Your wisdom, support, and prayers have shaped the educator and person I am today.

To my son, Timothy—your light, love, and unwavering encouragement have carried me through this journey. I am forever grateful for the joy, laughter, and inspiration you bring into my life.

To the ones who believed in my author dreams before I had the nerve to call myself a writer—thank you for seeing the book in me when I was just journaling in coffee shops and writing you letters. You know who you are, and I love you for it.

To every educator who's ever dreamed of having more life beyond the classroom—may you find laughter, validation, and maybe even a little peace within these pages.

This book is for you.

CONTENTS

Introduction

THE TEACHER'S DILEMMA

Ah, teaching! A thrilling career filled with loads of excitement and surprises around every corner. Bright lights and colors. Smiling faces. Lunchroom giggles layered with a few playground squeals. Hormones, crushes, and a splash of drama.

Teaching can be tons of fun. But if the world was a theme park, teaching would be that one roller coaster no one warned you about. You know, the one with the surprise drops, twists, and turns.

You start your career all fired up, ready to inspire the next generation of young minds. And it's beautiful. A class filled with the unfiltered joy of children. You get to witness little lightbulbs flickering as they learn new concepts. And when they turn completely on, that's the magic! You're surrounded by curiosity that evokes questions like "Why is the sky blue?", "Is there life on other planets?", and "Are you dating Coach Lewis?" Plus, how can you forget having weekends off, not having to work every major holiday on the calendar, and a summer break with pay? But somehow, despite all the wins, you end up drowning in papers, lost in lesson plans, and questioning your life choices by midyear. No one told you you'd have to be Wonder Woman, Batman, and every other member of the Justice League—all before lunch.

We all know teaching can be absolutely amazing, but it can also be extremely exhausting. There are days when you feel like a rock star, and then there are days when you're just . . . tired. And not that "oh, I didn't get enough sleep" tired. I mean deep-in-your-bones tired. What we in this profession call *teacher tired.*

And why wouldn't you be? You're not just a teacher—you're a counselor, mediator, parent, cheerleader, event planner, and part-time magician who's expected to pull miracles out of your ass . . . tonishing brain. I am in constant awe of the creativity, innovation, and magic we pull off daily. But just because we make it look like light work doesn't mean that everyone should expect us to be everything and everywhere all at once. The expectations in our profession are for us to create blockbuster lessons, differentiate instruction, collect data, attend after-school festivals, keep test scores up—all while keeping glorious smiles on our faces. Listen, I've got multiple degrees in education, and not one of them contained a course called Spirit Week 101 or Managing a Classroom Budget on Your Personal Funds. So if you're feeling the weight, I get it.

And guess what? This weight causes almost half of educators to leave the profession within their first five years. Teachers don't leave K–12 education because they hate it. They leave because burnout, stress, and emotional exhaustion are practically the fine print of the job description.

I know the toll that teaching can take firsthand. I've been deep in the trenches of education for the last twenty-four years. I started out teaching elementary school in a teeny, tiny town in Georgia. Like, everyone-knows-everyone small. Back then, I lived and breathed all things education. I loved my self-contained classes, where I could really get creative and connect with my students. At that point teaching was as fun as it was fulfilling, and I had all the energy in the world—until the realities of the job started creeping in, like admin doing an observation the day before a holiday.

You know the deal. The long hours. The never-ending grading. The constant need to be everything for everyone. Of course, I didn't recognize it at first. I chalked it up to me being a newbie, assuming that "things-to-do" list would eventually dwindle to nothing. But more and more, each year resembled the last.

I started to feel like I was running in circles trying to learn and teach ever-changing standards, all while trying to juggle students' varying academic strengths and emotional needs. Some of the kids in my classes were dealing with stuff that would break your heart. One child was always sleeping in class, and I later realized he was taking care of his siblings while his mother worked double shifts. I had another student who got caught stealing from the book fair, and the following week both of his parents were arrested for theft from a local grocery store, which resulted in him and his siblings being placed in foster care. And unfortunately, I have numerous accounts of abuse revealed through journal entries and private conversations. As a result, I ended up spending more time worrying about them than I did about my own life.

The stress of teaching doesn't end with classroom management either. Let's not forget the classroom budget. "What budget?" is actually more like it. If you're lucky, your school gives you a few hundred bucks on the first day of school, which is somehow supposed to fund the needs of twenty-five students for an entire year. And that's if you have a small self-contained class; depending on the grade level and structure of your school, some of you are teaching triple that amount. Crayons, glue sticks, scissors. Math manipulatives, science equipment, art materials. My credit card knows way too much about school supplies.

The budget crunch involved in education is so bad that parents donate sanitizer and antibacterial wipes to our Wish Lists (although we need to question why those supplies aren't included in the custodial budget). And we are all thankful for those room moms who donate to holiday parties and the occasional class activity.

However, the parent roster is a fifty-fifty toss-up. You never know who you're gonna get. And even if you have a room full of supportive parents, there are always a couple who are still capable of working your nerves. You know them—the helicopter parents who constantly hover, the business parent who treats you like an employee, and the wannabe lawyer who defends every incident, knowing good and dang well their child's middle name is *Rulebreaker*.

Through all of that stress, I still felt deep joy for teaching early in my career. After all, I was illuminating the way for the hundreds of students I taught. The downside was that the flames were burning at both ends of the candle, and I was getting scorched.

Fast-forward through getting married, having a baby, and obtaining a few higher degrees, and I found myself restless in my teacher role. I thought, "Maybe I can make a difference outside of the classroom," so I found a job in administration. My heart remained with my students and fellow teachers, but I also felt I could make a difference one policy at a time.

Ha! Little did I know, this new world of educational leadership would be filled with bureaucracy and politics. I started to question if I was still in the same profession. I remember pouring my heart into a curriculum I just knew would change the game—only to have it picked apart by people who cared more about checking boxes than actual learning. I also recall attending conferences with colleagues who excluded me from all associated functions. You know, the private meetings before or after the meeting. While I served several years in this role, it did not take long to realize I had unknowingly signed up for the ego Olympics. Some were there because they had worked hard, while others had slid in through a connection, but they were all competing to prove they deserved a seat at the table. And what were they doing at this table? You'd hope they were using their power to rid teachers of stress and solve students' academic issues. Unfortunately, many were heavily focused on angling for titles and cozying up to board members. And the wildest part was seeing the same behaviors I'd observed with teenagers: cliques, power trips, shady group chats. Talk about soul crushing.

I finally made my way back to the classroom—this time at a private middle school. I thought I'd found the spark again. And don't get me wrong, there were definitely aspects of greatness in my new teaching environment. The students were awesome, the energy was alive, but then . . . COVID happened. Teaching in the early days of COVID was like trying to entertain a room full of cats over Zoom. The screen was a barrier, student engagement decreased, and let's be honest: we were all just trying to survive.

When schools reopened, teachers immediately noticed a huge learning gap with the students we taught. Then, we all became part of a mythical race, trying to "catch kids up." What about their mental health? Heck, what about ours? Let's just say that the return to the classroom wasn't the reunion with teaching I had envisioned.

Whether or not you began teaching before, during, or after the pandemic, the epidemic of teacher burnout has always existed. Why? Well, I'll save all of my thoughts on the inequalities within a female-dominated profession. But I will say that burnout is prevalent in K–12 education primarily because teachers have subconsciously bought into the idea that it is their responsibility to maintain the lives of others while ignoring their own.

The whole "work-life balance" thing? It's a joke in this profession. People love to talk about "balance" like it's some Instagrammable concept. But when it comes to the average teacher, balance is about as real as a unicorn. We're out here nurturing other people's kids while neglecting our own lives—and that's not even a secret. With many schools, that sense of selflessness is expected. If you're a teacher, sacrificing your personal time is practically celebrated, like, "Wow, look at you going above and beyond with no compensation! Here's a week of jeans passes to celebrate you." Yes, an official out-of-uniform coupon for rocking denim.

That condescending presumption about my time and energy was where I finally had to draw the line. They kept piling things on my plate, like I didn't already have ten tabs open in my brain and three different crises in motion. I'd get pulled into last-minute meetings that could've been emails, asked to fix things that weren't my responsibility, and low-key guilt-tripped if I hesitated. And half the time, people barely acknowledged the extra work I was doing—they just assumed I'd keep showing up, smiling, and saving the day because that's what I signed up for, right? I should just be excited that someone gifted me with a snack. Like, was I really out here working for food? After years of being the go-to, overcommitting yes-person, I realized something had to give.

Battling Burnout

Once I stopped accepting the unrealistic—and unfair—expectations that I had wrongly internalized as part and parcel of working in education, I found that better life everyone talks about. You know, the one with balance, freedom, and peace of mind. Honey, it's actually out there—and it's a lot closer than you think.

You don't have to keep running on empty, waiting for a miracle. It's time to rediscover the joy that got you into teaching in the first place.

In this book, we're going to get real about setting boundaries, finding balance, and reconnecting with the passion that lights you up. We'll talk practical strategies (no fluff, just real talk), personal stories (because, trust me, I've been where you are), and some advice to help you thrive—and not just survive.

- **Lesson One:** Boundaries are your friend. If you're not careful, this job will take every last ounce of energy you've got. And it'll leave you there, drained and wondering where it all went. But setting those boundaries means protecting yourself from burnout. It's knowing that you don't have to attend every event, respond to every late-night email, or be the savior of every struggling student on your own.

- **Lesson Two:** Know your worth and act on it. This isn't just about getting paid what you deserve (although yes, please, ask for that raise or stipend). It's also about valuing your time, your energy, and the impact you have on students' lives. Recognize that your work is *important*, and so is the time you spend recharging.
- **Lesson Three:** Teaching doesn't mean you have to sacrifice your life. You deserve hobbies, joy, weekends with friends, dates, and family dinners that aren't interrupted by a text from school. We can be devoted to our students without losing ourselves in the process. It's all about balance—finding that sweet spot where work and life coexist without one overshadowing the other.
- **Lesson Four:** Embrace change. Sometimes what worked once just doesn't anymore. You grow, your needs change, and it's okay to leave situations that no longer serve you. Teaching is a calling, but it doesn't mean you're glued to the classroom or a specific position forever. Sometimes, the most powerful thing you can do is let go.

Embracing these foundational lessons is not just a personal decision. It is a deeply personal act of liberation. We live in a world that expects internet-speed responses, instant solutions, and 24-7 availability, but you are not a robot. You are not AI. You have a body that tires, a mind that needs rest, and a heart that yearns for joy outside of your job title.

It is essential to know your value and not equate it with how accessible you are to everyone else. Understanding balance is about being intentional with your yeses, and in doing so, you teach others—students, colleagues, and sometimes even yourself—that well-being is not optional. It is the foundation for sustainable service. And the more you protect your peace, the more powerful your presence becomes.

Knowing your self-worth then becomes a daily practice, a quiet resistance against systems that applaud exhaustion and confuse sacrifice with dedication. You will begin to see your value in the depth you contribute and not how much of yourself you give away. For me, I had to realize that I bring a level of skill, intuition, and leadership that can't be replicated. Therefore, I honor my worth to create alignment with myself.

It's not that I love the work any less. (In fact, I love it more!) I just finally understand love shouldn't cost me everything. I embrace change, even when it's uncomfortable, because I know now that growth requires movement. As I redefine success, I start to imagine a world where educators thrive instead of survive. Where students learn from teachers who are living examples of balance, joy, and resilience. Where school is not a place of depletion, but a space of restoration—for everyone. This is more than a philosophy; it's a call to shift culture. Because when I protect my wholeness, I give others permission to do the same. And maybe that's how transformation really begins—with one teacher being the change.

That vision of work-life balance may sound too good to be true, but this book is designed to get you there through achievable, empowering steps that you can take every day in and, importantly, out of the classroom. Accordingly, this book is broken down into three parts that cover three major goals of achieving work-life balance.

Part 1: Protecting Your Mental Health and Personal Time covers the crucial first step: changing your mind-set toward teaching. Throughout Part 1, the chapters will guide you in developing the tools to set healthy boundaries without guilt, empowering you to say "no" with confidence and clarity. Each chapter builds on the idea that preserving your well-being is not only possible but essential, offering practical strategies to reclaim your time, shift away from people-pleasing habits, and rediscover a sense of calm and inner balance in both your personal and professional life.

Part 2: Building Sustainable Work Habits covers everyday interventions that will allow you to take control of your work life so that it better suits everyone's needs—including, most importantly, your own. Over the course of Part 2, we'll discuss ways to reclaim and own your time, simplify your workload by working smarter, and establish routines that are sustainable. It's about creating systems that support you—not drain you—so you can thrive in your day-to-day.

Finally, Part 3: Reconnecting with Your Passion for Teaching dives into strategies for reconnecting with the spark that first lit your imagination as a teacher—and for sustaining the hearth fire that will ultimately keep you going. As we close, we'll take a walk down memory lane as we remember the "why" that brought us to this profession. We will learn how to embrace and cultivate joy in the classroom and learn how teaching from a place of balance and fulfillment ultimately makes us better educators.

As you take this journey with me, I hope you begin to see that your well-being is just as vital as your work. I want you to love yourself as deeply as you love your profession. I want you to feel empowered to mentally and physically clock out, without guilt or fear, knowing that rest is part of the rhythm of great teaching. My hope is that these ideas spark a personal transformation—one that shifts your mind-set, reshapes your habits, and reclaims your joy. But even more than that, I hope this becomes a quiet revolution, one that improves not only your quality of life but also the impact you have on your students and the quality of work you bring to the classroom. Together, we can create a new standard—where thriving, not surviving, becomes the norm in education.

Because here's the thing: you deserve to be a great teacher and live a fulfilling life. And no, you don't have to choose one or the other. Being an educator does not mean you have to commit to a 24-7 shift. Remember, you are a teacher by day.

Part 1

PROTECTING YOUR MENTAL HEALTH AND PERSONAL TIME

Chapter 1

THE IMPORTANCE OF BOUNDARIES

See, What Had Happened Was: I Gave the Wrong Parent My Number

There was a time in my career that I used to give parents my personal number like I was Oprah handing out cars. "You get access! And you get access!" Yeah, yeah, yeah, I now know this was a horrible idea. But, in my defense, all those handy number-concealing apps were not yet invented. I thought this level of availability was going to help us become closer, make communication easier—you know, "build bridges" and all that. Honey, I built a bridge straight to destruction.

Now, at first, the messages from parents seemed harmless. Sure, they meant I was thinking about school a lot more. Those quick texts like, "Did Keisha leave her coat in class?" still keep you in teacher mode. And nothing prevents your brain from truly shutting down like a random text about a missing homework assignment, which leads to a request to send a copy of the worksheet. But the real drama went down when I chose not to respond to one particular parent after 10 p.m.

This parent? Let's call her Mrs. Unbothered-by-Your-Personal-Life. One random school night, I decided to ignore this parent's text. I was exhausted, it was late, and no one needs to be texting me after 10 p.m. unless the school's on fire. And, even then, it can wait, because do I look like the fire department? I told myself I'd respond the next morning.

As soon as the bell rang the next morning, Mrs. Unbothered strolled into my room with the attitude turned up to a thousand. "I texted you last night! So I guess you're not planning to respond?" she snapped. "Oh, we're doing this? Before 8 a.m.? In front of the kids?" I thought. I calmly asked her to step into the hallway because there were twenty little faces staring at me. And I was not about to go full *Real Housewives* in front of them.

I explained to this parent that I wasn't obligated to respond to texts outside of work hours, and that's when it hit me: This was kinda my fault. I gave these parents an all-access pass to my life, like I was on call 24-7. And now they were used to it, conditioned to think I was always available. And let me tell you, snatching that privilege back was like trying to take a lollipop from a toddler. Baby, it was not pretty.

I thought giving my parents access made me look dedicated, noble even, and honestly, I craved their admiration. I wanted parents to respect me so much they'd name their next kid after me. But let me tell you—when I got a 10:42 p.m. email asking why their child only got a 93 instead of a 100, I realized I confused being available with being valuable. And honey, those are not the same thing.

The thing is, some parents see teachers as customer service reps for their child's academic experience. Like, I'm the manager of a twenty-four-hour Homework Hotline and they're Yelp reviewers equipped with a Wi-Fi signal and entitlement. Sis. Sir. Neither your tax dollars nor tuition purchased a round-the-clock tutor. These expectations aren't just unfair. They're self-centered, and they erase the fact that I'm a whole human with a whole life. I have bills, doctor appointments, a Trader Joe's run, maybe a date if the stars align. I am not just Miss So-and-So or a teaching machine. I am a full person who teaches.

So let's shift this whole mindset. Teachers are not educational genies living in a standards-based lamp. We are professionals, not possessions. We deserve boundaries, rest, and the basic human right to eat dinner without being interrogated about Johnny's missing book log. Respect doesn't come from constant availability—it comes from mutual recognition of humanity. I teach with the whole child in mind, and I expect the same in return. So let's retire the myth that the best teachers give all of themselves all the time. Because when we teach from a place of wholeness, everybody wins. Even little Johnny. Especially little Johnny.

Now I set clear boundaries from day one. At the beginning of the year, I communicate my availability in a welcome letter and at Open House. I share when and how I can be contacted—usually during school hours via email—and I stick to it. I've found that when I'm proactive and consistent with these expectations, parents actually respect them more.

The real shift happened when I stopped reacting and started leading. Instead of waiting for problems to arise, I created a system of regular communication—weekly updates, newsletters, and scheduled conferences—that kept parents informed without draining me. I set an expectation where communication was purposeful, not constant. This new approach not only protected my time and energy, but it also set the tone for the kind of classroom culture I wanted: one rooted in clarity, respect, and mutual support. I learned that boundaries aren't walls—they're bridges built with intention. And by modeling healthy boundaries, I give parents permission to do the same in their own lives.

That experience with parents taught me a deeper truth: Boundaries aren't just for managing communication—they're essential for sustaining joy and longevity in this profession. Once I realized how powerful it was to set clear expectations with families, I started applying the same principle across the board—with colleagues, students, and even myself. I stopped saying yes to every last-minute favor, every after-school event, and some happy hours. Instead, I began asking myself, "Is this aligned with my values and energy right now?" If the answer was no, I gracefully bowed out. Boundaries are a form of self-respect, and they give others a model of what healthy professionalism looks like.

Moral of the story? Set your boundaries and communicate them up front. Because once you hand out that backstage pass to your life, it's hard to revoke without some drama.

Why Setting Boundaries Is Crucial for Your Mental Health

Boundaries are a teacher's secret weapon, especially *if you're seeking a more balanced life.* As an educator, you've already figured out that teaching is not just a job—it's a full-on, in-your-face, 24-7 emotional marathon that will chew you up, spit you out, and leave you wondering why you voluntarily subject yourself to the madness—but only if you let it.

Don't get me wrong, we love our students. I mean, we usually spend more waking hours with them than anyone else. We bond over story time, recess play, and teenage drama. And we live for those "Aha!" moments when a kid finally gets a skill you've been teaching for days.

But let's not pretend like the love for teaching isn't a double-edged sword. It pulls us in so deep that sometimes we forget one simple truth: We are not superheroes. We don't have capes or unlimited energy, and we shouldn't be expected to carry the weight of an entire system on our backs. What we do have, though, is the power to reclaim control over our lives—if we choose to. Think of the lessons in this book as your personal Infinity Stones, each one helping you master a different dimension of your teaching life.

Just like in the Marvel universe, each Infinity Stone represents a force of power: space, reality, time, mind, power, and soul. In our world, *space* is the physical and mental room you give yourself to breathe. *Reality* is the honest look at what you need to thrive. *Time* is how you manage your hours without burning out. *Mind* is your clarity, focus, and emotional balance. *Power* is the ability to say "no" without apology, and *soul* is the joy and purpose that brought you to teaching in the first place.

When you learn to hold and use these stones intentionally—through boundaries, balance, and bold self-leadership—you stop surviving and start living fully. You don't need to be a superhero. You just need the right tools—and the courage to use them.

If you've been teaching for more than a minute, you've already heard the phrase "You don't teach for the income, you teach for the outcome." It's cute, right? Except for it's really some kind of Jedi mind trick that brainwashes us into sacrificing every single thing about ourselves for the job in an attempt to earn this invisible badge of honor. And who else is out here working without an income in mind? Miss me with that, because that, my friends, is where we get it twisted.

For most of us, teaching is not just a job; it becomes an identity. We call our students "our kids," fully aware that none of them came out of our wombs (or our . . . well, you get the point). And we mean it. We'll stand up for them, show up for them, and give them everything we can. We care that much.

And while that commitment to our students sounds heartwarming on the surface, it's also the exact reason why so many of us feel stretched way too thin. Because somewhere along the line, we got the idea that being a "good teacher" means saying yes to everything: working late nights, grading papers until we fall asleep with red ink on our hands, and spending our own money to make sure our classrooms look warm and inviting.

So why do we do this to ourselves? Why do we keep giving and giving until we have nothing left? Because we care. And that's beautiful, but it's also dangerous. When you constantly give without taking time to recharge, the stress piles up. And before you know it, you're feeling burned-out, run-down, and questioning whether this is what you want to be doing with your life.

According to a 2025 University of Missouri study reported by the *National Education Association*, 78 percent of teachers have considered quitting due to burnout from limited support, heavy workloads, low pay, and student challenges.[1] And honestly? I get it. While our students' joy and accomplishments are rewarding, most of us are walking around here with a backpack of stress weighing us down.

The good news is you don't have to carry it all. You really don't. There is power in dropping the stuff that doesn't serve you. You're still a phenomenal teacher when you protect your peace. Actually, you might be even better.

Setting boundaries allows us to keep from crashing. Boundaries are not just about protecting your time, but also about protecting your energy and mental health. Think of them as a protective shield between you and all the things that could drain you dry. Boundaries are the difference between giving your students the best and giving your students whatever's left of you. A teacher who's running on fumes isn't doing anybody any favors—not themselves, not their students, and definitely not their loved ones.

The Common Pitfalls of Overcommitting

Teachers—especially the ones who *care*—are notorious for stretching ourselves so thin that, by the time summer rolls around, we're not even relaxing; we're just *recovering*. Let's examine a few of the biggest culprits of overcommitting and some ways to set healthier boundaries instead.

1 Walker, Tim. "What's Causing Teacher Burnout?" *NEA Today*, National Education Association, April 7, 2025, www.nea.org/nea-today/all-news-articles/whats-causing-teacher-burnout.

1. Parent Communication: When to Put Your Email on "Do Not Disturb"

Ah, parent emails. Nothing says "boundary violation" quite like getting an email from a parent at 11 p.m. on a Sunday asking why Matthew got a B on his essay (that, by the way, he barely even wrote). And even worse? You sit there, debating whether to respond right then, thinking, "If I don't, they'll think I'm ignoring them."

Let me say this plainly: You are not on call 24-7. Parents do not need access to you at all hours of the day and night. You are allowed to have a life, a dinner, a Netflix binge—whatever you need to unwind. Your email inbox will still be there in the morning.

Here's the move: At the beginning of the year, set clear expectations around communication. Let parents know that you're available during school hours and maybe for a short period after, but that outside of those times you're not checking email or answering calls. If they have an emergency, there are other school staff they can contact.

At Open House I walk everyone through my class syllabus—what we're learning, how I grade, when I respond, and what I don't do. This is when I insert examples, such as responding to emails after hours. I also hit their inbox with a friendly welcome email with a recap of those points.

Just like the kids, the parents are going to test the boundaries, so be ready to gently remind them with consistency. I keep a quirky "Out of Office" auto-reply ready to go. Something like, "Hey, y'all! I'm currently away from my inbox, probably on a walk in the city or eating dinner with my family. I'll get back to you within twenty-four business hours. Thanks for your patience." It sets the tone and reminds them that I'm professional, I'm human, and I've got boundaries that help me be the best version of myself—for their kids and mine.

This boundary around parent communication is a game changer. You don't need to be tethered to your inbox like it's a life-support machine. Put that thing on "Do Not Disturb" after hours and enjoy your life.

2. Classroom Preparation: The Pinterest Trap

We've seen the teachers with the matching color schemes, the carefully curated reading nooks, the desks arranged using an educational feng shui that could make Marie Kondo jealous. And we all want our classrooms to look like that viral video our favorite teacher influencer posted last week.

But let's get one thing straight: Classroom aesthetics don't teach the kids anything. You know what does? You. Your lesson plans, your passion, your energy, your ability to make learning come alive. So the next time you find yourself deep in a Pinterest spiral, trying to decide between boho-chic or industrial-modern decor, pause. Remind yourself that a beautifully decorated classroom is great, but it's not the be-all, end-all.

Sure, it's fun to decorate, and I'm not saying your classroom should look like a sad blank slate. But know your limits. You don't need to spend all weekend rearranging desks for "maximum coziness" or spend your paycheck on fairy lights to make a whimsical learning environment. Put up a few things that make you happy, set the mood, and then stop. It's okay to have a classroom that's functional rather than a work of art.

3. Lesson Planning: When "Good Enough" Is Actually Good Enough

Let me say this louder for the perfectionists in the back: *Every single lesson does not need to be a showstopper!* I know, I know—you want each lesson to be memorable. You want your students to leave class every day like, "Wow, Ms. Johnson just blew my mind. Again."

But here's the truth: Not every lesson is going to change lives. And that's okay.

Some lessons will be average. Some will be downright boring. (I said what I said.) But as long as the kids are learning, it's okay. You don't need to be at your creative peak for every single class. You're not Picasso. You're not even Bob Ross, painting his happy little trees on PBS. And honestly, that's fine.

I remember spending hours—I mean, *hours*—on lesson plans that I thought were going to knock my students' socks off. I would research, design, tweak, and perfect intricate activities, only to have half the class stare blankly at me while the other half was more interested in the clock than in the beautifully crafted handouts I spent all night on.

Save your energy for the big moments and give yourself permission to throw in a straightforward, no-frills lesson every now and then. Trust me, your students will be just fine. And it'll make the elaborate moments more special.

Planning an elaborate lesson, like a classroom makeover, can be worth it when the effort both strengthens students' understanding of a difficult concept and builds energy and camaraderie. For example, during my *Romeo and Juliet* unit, I transform my room into a medieval Verona and divide the class into Capulets and Montagues. It helps students better grasp Shakespeare's world while role-playing scenes to deepen their comprehension. Similarly, for March Madness math, when students compete in bracket-style tournaments solving algebra problems, the basketball court decor fuels healthy competition, makes practice fun, and reinforces key skills.

4. Grading: Sometimes a Smiley Face Will Do

Grading is another black hole that will swallow up your evenings and weekends if you let it. I used to believe that every paper needed to be graded with detailed comments, helpful suggestions, and insightful feedback on every single word. Like I was some kind of grading Yoda, handing out wisdom one essay at a time.

Ain't nobody got time for that.

Listen, I know we all want to be that teacher who leaves detailed feedback on every paper like, "Riley, your thesis statement was great, but you need a stronger analysis." But are these kids even reading your heartfelt critiques? And if they are, will they really know how to develop a "stronger analysis" just because we wrote it? Probably not.

Instead of bleeding red ink, look for trends. Maybe you notice half the class still thinks a paragraph is a sentence and the other half is allergic to textual evidence. Jot those issues down. At the end, pull your Top Five Hot-Mess Moments—boom, you've just built a whole week's worth of focused mini-lessons. Less hand cramping for you, more real learning for them. Just remember that if it's important enough for you to assign an assessment, then it's important enough to prioritize grading it. Period. As a result, I slot it into my weekly schedule just like I would a team meeting.

When students get their work back quickly, they have time to reflect, adjust, and get better. My rule of thumb? Multiple-choice quizzes should have a one- to two-day turnaround. (And if you're using something electronic that grades itself? Baby, that's same-day, no excuses.) Short answers? Give yourself three days, tops—especially if you're teaching multiple classes. Essays or mathematical equations that require the examination of steps in various handwriting should be ready no more than a week from the last day it was due.

If you're spending hours grading every night and weekends are dedicated to catching up on assessments, it's time to reevaluate your system. Here's a secret: Most kids don't care if you wrote, "I loved your metaphor about the ocean being a reflection of the human soul." "Nice imagery!" will work just fine. Keep feedback simple, keep it clear, and for the love of all things caffeinated, stop grading everything. Your sanity will thank you.

5. Extracurricular Activities: The Slippery Slope of "Just One More Thing"

Let's talk about extracurriculars, because I know y'all aren't just teaching. You're also coaching, advising, chaperoning, attending after-school meetings, and showing up at every school event like you've got a clone handling your home life.

I know it's tempting to say yes when your principal asks if you can "just help out" with one more club or committee. I mean, you *could* do it. You're competent. You're probably even a little flattered they asked. But you also need to know when to say no.

Here's the thing: Every "yes" you give at work is a "no" somewhere else in your life. Every "yes" is time you're not spending with your family, your friends, or—heaven forbid—yourself. So the next time someone asks you to chaperone a dance or run the student council, stop and ask yourself an important question: "Do I really have the time and energy for this?"

While a "no" may be the best answer to extracurricular activities, there are times when a "yes" could be beneficial. I see these opportunities as investments. If the work is attached to a nice stipend, I'm likely to agree. Other reasons to say yes would include alignment with your passions, if it fits into your life without wrecking your health or home time, or if it can help you grow a skill or strengthen your résumé for a bigger end goal.

For example, if you're thinking about moving into leadership, activities like running a club, coaching a team, or organizing an event could be the kind of hands-on experience that sets you apart later. It's about being intentional with your decision-making. If it feeds your energy, future, or bank account, it could be worth your time. If not, politely pass. You're building a career, not just collecting gold stars.

If the answer is no, it's perfectly okay to say no. You don't need to be Superteacher, doing all the things and saving the day. Pick one or two things you enjoy, do them well, and politely pass on the rest.

How to Set Those Boundaries without Feeling Like the "Bad Guy"

Now that we've established five areas where you likely need to establish boundaries, let's talk about how to actually set them. Because if you're like me, the mere thought of telling someone no makes you break out in a cold sweat. It feels rude, or worse, like you're letting people down. But news flash: Setting boundaries isn't about being the bad guy, it's about protecting your peace.

Here are a few tips on how to set boundaries with the people of your professional world:

1. Boundaries with Your Students

Students are great, but they can also be little boundary pushers if you let them. They'll come to you before school, during lunch, after school, and on the weekends. Some of them will try to hit you up on social media—don't fall for it, or before you know it, you'll become their on-demand tutor.

The key with students is setting clear communication rules up front. Let them know when you're available and when you're not. For example, maybe you tell them that you're there for help during lunch or after school on certain days, but evenings and weekends are off-limits.

You can also use what I like to call the "parking lot method": Create a designated space in the classroom where students can leave nonurgent questions. One easy way to set this up is by putting a small basket or a box near the door with sticky notes and pens. Students can jot down their questions and drop them in throughout the day. For a digital option, older students can use a free online tool like Padlet or even just send an email. I like to take the last five minutes of class to pull a few questions from the "parking lot" and answer them out loud—because usually if one student is wondering about something, several others are too. This system keeps students from interrupting you during your much-needed personal time and gives you a controlled, scheduled way to support them without feeling overwhelmed.

2. Boundaries with the Parents

Parents love their kids, and sometimes that love manifests as extreme overinvolvement in your classroom. But that doesn't mean they should have 24-7 access to you.

At the start of the year, set communication boundaries with parents too. Let them know the best way to reach you (email, phone, an app like Remind) and when you're available to respond. If a parent calls you at 9 p.m. on a Saturday, it's okay to let that call go to voice mail and return it during work hours.

Also, get comfortable with having a script for tricky conversations. You know the ones—where parents ask you to do something you just don't have the time or energy for. A simple "I appreciate your concern, and I will address it when I can" works wonders.

3. Boundaries with Your Colleagues

Colleagues can be your greatest supporters, but they can also be a source of pressure when it comes to taking on more work. The cycle of saying yes to every committee, every after-school event, and every collaborative project can feel like a badge of honor. But we all know it can be exhausting.

When a colleague approaches you with another "great opportunity," take a moment before you respond. Ask yourself:

- Do I have the time?
- Is this aligned with my goals?
- Would I say yes if it weren't for a sense of obligation?

If the answer to any of these questions is a firm no, don't be afraid to say it. It's important to be strategic with how you turn colleagues down. You can respond with something like, "I'd love to help out, but I'm at my limit right now. Maybe next time?" This way, you're not closing the door entirely, but you're also being honest about your current capacity. It's all about prioritizing your well-being while still being supportive of your team.

4. Boundaries with Admin

Let's not kid ourselves—admin can have their own set of expectations that often feel overwhelming. Whether it's last-minute requests for reports or attending meetings that could have been emails, navigating the waters of administrative demands requires a delicate balance.

To place boundaries with admin, start by establishing a clear line of communication. If something feels unreasonable, don't hesitate to express your concerns professionally. For example, if you're being asked to attend yet another meeting during your planning period, it's perfectly okay to say, "I really value these meetings, but my planning time is crucial for my students' success. Is there a way we can streamline this?"

You can also set boundaries around how often you check emails or respond to requests. Renegotiating expectations from admin is about finding a mutual respect that allows you to perform your duties effectively without sacrificing your mental health.

When Boundaries Are Tested

So you've taken the plunge and started setting boundaries. But then, suddenly, a wave of demands crashes down on you like a bad hair day in a windstorm. What do you do when the universe seems to be testing those hard-earned boundaries? Here are some strategies to help you navigate those moments.

1. Pause and Reflect

When you feel overwhelmed, take a step back and breathe. Ground yourself in the present. Ask yourself what's causing your stress. Is it a specific request? A lack of time? External pressures? Acknowledging what's happening can help you clarify your priorities and move forward with a plan of response.

2. Prioritize Your Tasks

Not every task is created equal. Use the Eisenhower Matrix to categorize tasks into four quadrants:

- Urgent and Important: Do these now.
- Important, but Not Urgent: Schedule these.
- Urgent, but Not Important: Delegate if possible.
- Neither Urgent nor Important: Eliminate these.

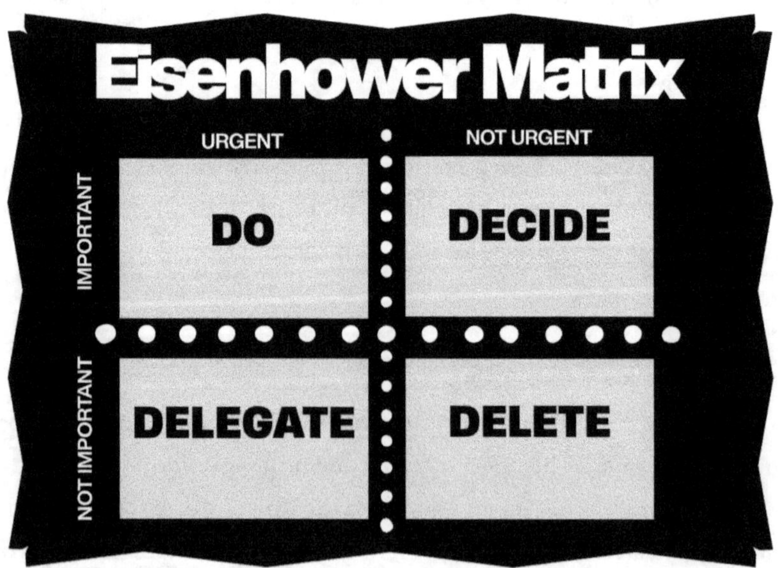

Here's an example of how you can use the Eisenhower Matrix at the end of the semester when everything is coming at you like dodgeballs.

Grading final exams? Urgent and Important—no debate. Writing recommendation letters that aren't due yet? Important but Not Urgent. Schedule some chill time to knock those out. That random student email asking about next year's electives? Urgent but Not Important. Pass it to the department head or a counselor. Spending two hours bedazzling your door for a spirit contest? That's Neither Urgent nor Important. Unless it feeds your soul, leave it alone.

By prioritizing your tasks, you can focus your energy where it matters most and alleviate some of the pressure that comes from feeling pulled in too many directions. We'll discuss more strategies for streamlining and organizing your teaching workload in Part 2.

3. Seek Support

You don't have to navigate the demands of teaching all alone. Reach out to friends, family, or fellow teachers when you feel overwhelmed. Sometimes just talking it out can give you a new perspective, and other people might have solutions you haven't considered.

4. Reassess Your Boundaries

If you find yourself repeatedly overwhelmed despite your efforts to set boundaries, it may be time to reassess your boundaries. Are they realistic? Are you adhering to them? It's okay to adjust your limits as your situation changes.

One time, I decided to stretch a boundary—and honestly, I'm glad I did. I signed up to chaperone a four-day field trip to Orlando with three hundred students. Was it exhausting? *Absolutely.* Constant head counts, long lines, chasing teenagers through theme parks, running on way too much caffeine and not enough sleep—it was a lot. But the pros stacked up fast. I got to really connect with students, laughing with them and seeing who they were outside of the classroom. I also built strong bonds with other teachers, the kind that only come from surviving roller coasters and epic missions to track down students' lost cell phones together. Plus, I had fun. Being new to the school, it was the best crash course I could've asked for to understand the community and feel like part of the team. Will I sign up again? Maybe, maybe not. But either way, it was a total win—proof that sometimes stretching a boundary just a little brings more connection, memories, and joy than you ever expected.

5. Practice Self-Care

Finally, self-care is not just a buzzword; it's essential. Make sure you're carving out time for activities that rejuvenate you, whether that's reading a book or going for a walk. Your well-being impacts your ability to be present for your students, so prioritize self-care as a nonnegotiable part of your routine.

The Power of Community: Building Your Support Network

You don't have to set boundaries alone. Building a community of supportive colleagues and friends can make a world of difference in maintaining your boundaries. Building strong community with other educator colleagues gives you a support system that *normalizes* setting and respecting boundaries, so you don't feel like the "bad guy" for protecting your time. It also creates accountability. When others are modeling healthy habits too, it's easier (and less awkward) to stick to your own. Here's how you can cultivate that community:

1. Connect with Like-Minded Colleagues

Find those teachers who get it—the ones who understand the struggles of the classroom and the importance of boundaries. Create a network where you can share experiences, vent frustrations, and offer advice. Professional connections can help you feel less isolated and more empowered.

Right now, someone reading this book is saying, "You *clearly* don't know my team!" And you're right, I don't. But honey, I've worked with colleagues whom I prayed would retire or find a new job just to decrease the negativity in the building. I get it.

Sometimes feeling isolated at school isn't because there's nobody around—it's because the people around you aren't *your people*. You've got veteran teachers side-eyeing the newbies, newbies too scared to ask for help, and Negative Nancys turning every meeting into a therapy session nobody asked for. Then there's the old-school folks clinging to "the way we've always done it" like it's a life raft, and the "my way or the highway" types who act like collaboration is a hostage situation. And don't even get me started on the secret-society vibe at super competitive schools, where sharing ideas feels like handing out cheat codes to the enemy. It's not loneliness, it's survival.

Still, you don't have to be alone in this. The magic of the Internet is literally at your fingertips. You have the chance to build a community with like-minded teachers across the globe. So while any reader can use the next two ideas, know that I wrote them especially for the teachers feeling isolated in their school environments.

2. Think Global: Make Connections Outside Your Bubble

Your go-to teacher buddy doesn't have to be in your building or even in your country! Teaching challenges are universal, and you'll find teachers worldwide who are going through the same struggles. Join a group on Facebook or even WhatsApp. You'll be surprised at how quickly "across the pond" connections start to feel like "across the hall" ones.

3. Slide into the Right DMs

Whether you're into X, Instagram, or LinkedIn, reach out to real, down-to-earth teachers who teach similar subjects, have a style you vibe with, or are just as passionate as you are. Don't limit yourself to the teachers with a million followers (they're probably busy syncing music to their next Reel, anyway). Instead, find teachers with smaller followings but real experience. Follow a few hashtags like #TeachInHarmony, #TeachersFollowTeachers, or #EducatorsUnited. Don't hesitate to hit someone up in their DMs to talk lesson ideas or swap strategies.

4. Find an Accountability Partner

Having someone to check in with can be a game changer. An accountability partner can help you stay on track with your goals and remind you to stick to your boundaries when the temptation to overcommit arises. If you can find multiple accountability partners, even better. But one can play multiple roles.

An accountability partnership in education is like being on a sports team, but with way less sweat. You've got your cheerleader hyping you up when you're killing it and keeping you motivated, and your referee ready to throw a flag when you're about to let your boundaries slip. Then there are your teammates—some are guarding your time like it's the final seconds of the game and some are stepping up to take the ball and handle things when you need to tag out. And don't forget the coach—they're there to help you strategize, collaborate, and make sure you're running the plays that keep you in the game without burning out. It's all about having a squad that's got your back, keeping it real, and making sure everyone stays on track.

5. Celebrate Each Other's Wins

Take the time to celebrate each other's successes, no matter how small. A simple "You did an amazing job on that project!" can reinforce the positive behaviors we want to cultivate in ourselves and each other.

The Takeaways

Let's break it down so you can protect your peace and your energy:

Support Your Mental Health

- Boundaries are the line between thriving and burning out. Setting clear limits protects your mental health and helps you show up as your best self, in and out of the classroom.

Avoid the Overstretch

- Teachers often stretch ourselves thin by answering late-night emails, taking on extra duties, staying late to finish work, or saying yes to every request. Identifying these areas is the first step in creating boundaries.

Build Healthy Boundaries

- Set clear rules about communication and behavior while remaining approachable. Be professional but firm about your availability and practice saying no when your plate is full. Above all, advocate for yourself.

Boundaries are the ultimate act of self-care, and when you set them, you teach others how to respect you while also creating space for a more balanced and fulfilling life.

At the end of the day, remember that setting boundaries doesn't mean shutting people out. It means prioritizing your well-being so you can show up as your best self for your students, your colleagues, and yourself. Boundaries are not barriers; they're bridges to healthier relationships and a more fulfilling career.

So embrace the power of "no," and remember that you're allowed to have a life outside of teaching. You deserve it, and your students will benefit from a happier, healthier you.

Chapter 2

SAYING "NO" WITHOUT GUILT

See, What Had Happened Was: I Said "No" with My Chest

If you've ever changed schools during your career, you know the pressure that comes with building your reputation. Sure, *you* know you arrive at a new school with experience, awards, and recommendations, but everyone in that building has to see you in action to believe it.

This was the case when I started at a new school midway into my career. Everything was exciting, and teaching the students was a piece of cake. Still, I was drowning in a sea of lesson plans (a task my former administrator didn't require) and feeling the anxiety from the impending deadlines of new-hire paperwork and district training. I wanted to say yes to everything, thinking that willingness to show up and contribute would magically transform me into the educational superstar I wanted everyone to see, but something inside of me kept whispering, "Nooooo, don't dooooo iiiiiittt."

One day my principal called me into his office. "I have a fantastic opportunity for you!" he said with a sparkle in his eye. "We're starting a cohort for gifted certification, and I think you'd be perfect for it."

Every teacher knows it takes a lot to earn respect in our profession. Without titles or accolades, we are often perceived as glorified babysitters. And that's not a good look. So even though I had years under my belt, I knew that being new to this school placed me back at the starting line. My inner monologue was all over the place: "Yes! A chance to shine! Wait, how much work is this going to be? You don't wanna look lazy, do you? But what if I drop the ball?" It was like a tug-of-war match with my aspirations on one side and my sanity on the other.

So being the overzealous new teacher I was, I said, "Absolutely! Sign me up!" Because what's the harm in adding one more thing to my already overflowing plate? Cue the dramatic music, because I was about to learn that saying yes has some major consequences.

As the days turned into weeks, the reality of my decision hit hard. I was expected to juggle after-school duties, attend meetings during my planning period, and complete assignments for this Gifted Certification program. I mean, it was a scheduling nightmare! When was I supposed to breathe, let alone work on my normal teaching responsibilities?

I felt like a contestant on *Survivor: Teacher Edition*. The stress was building, and soon I found myself knee-deep in frustration. I was overwhelmed, but there was a little voice in my head that kept whispering, "Girl, you need to speak up."

So I gathered my courage, put on my best "professional" face, and asked for a sit-down with my principal. I was nervous, but I had to tell him the truth. "I appreciate the opportunity for the Gifted Certification," I told him, "but I genuinely don't have the capacity to handle everything. The after-school duties and meetings during my planning period are leaving me with no time to focus on the coursework or even my teaching prep. In order to be successful, I need something removed."

To my surprise, my principal didn't look shocked. Instead, he nodded thoughtfully. I expected him to launch into a motivational speech about dedication or how we have to make sacrifices. But instead, he said, "Let's adjust your schedule. I can remove your extra duties so you can focus on your certification work." Um, excuse me? Did I just hear that correctly? I felt like I'd just discovered the secret menu at my favorite taco spot. Just like that, all duties—car duty, recess duty, and occasional afternoon meetings—were removed. By simply expressing my concerns, I was able to reclaim my time and sanity.

It turned out that saying no wasn't the terrifying monster I had built it up to be. Instead, it was a necessary strategy that led to more balance in my life. I walked out of that meeting feeling like I'd just slayed a dragon.

Because I was able to say no, I had the time to dive into my Gifted Certification course without sacrificing my sanity. Also, that "no" gave me the courage to respond appropriately to similar situations that quickly followed.

We often wish for more hours in the day, yet we hand the ones we already have away freely like samples at Costco. Sometimes saying "no" opens doors you didn't even know were closed. Imagine using that time to take a walk, read a book, or take a nap (yes, a nap). Listen, we are navigating the wild world of teaching and are worthy of all the time we can get. When you know your worth (and add tax), you stop discounting your time for things that don't align with your purpose, peace, or personal joy.

So next time you're faced with an opportunity that feels too heavy to carry, channel your inner badass and remember that saying no is just another way of saying yes to yourself.

The Compelling Need to Say Yes

If there's one thing teachers are basically Olympic athletes at, it's saying "yes." You want me to tutor during lunch? Count me in! Organize the school dance? Oh, absolutely! Chaperone the field trip? You know it! It's like we believe we're receiving a gold star in heaven every time we agree to take on a new task.

I would be willing to bet many of you feel like a boulder of guilt has been dropped on your chest the moment you even *think* about saying "no." Sadly, you're not alone. As teachers, we've got a superpower to empathize with, like, the entire universe. We care so much that it's like we're running a one-man show of compassion. Students, colleagues, parents, that random stranger in the coffee shop who looks like they're having a rough day—we feel *all* of it. And it's cute at first, you know? Being that generous, supportive soul starts out virtuous. But then, it starts getting real toxic, real quick.

Let's be real. Saying "yes" feels amazing. It's like biting into a warm, gooey, fresh-from-the-oven chocolate chip cookie. That hit of sweetness on your tastebuds makes you think, "Yes! Best decision ever!" But you know what happens when you keep downing those cookies, right? You end up sluggish, full of regret, and low-key wondering why you ever thought this was a good idea. Sound familiar?

Of course, saying "yes" can build connections, open doors to new opportunities, and reinforce a sense of generosity—especially when aligned with your values. It can also deepen relationships, expand your comfort zone, and sometimes lead to unexpected growth, joy, or collaboration. But often, because teaching comes without the praise some of us need, that "yes" gives us the applause we crave.

See, the thing is, our brains are wired to crave approval, and saying "yes" is like a fast pass to getting that hit of dopamine. Dopamine is the feel-good chemical that gives you a boost every time you do something people praise. So when you agree to run that extra meeting, take on another after-school program, or chaperone at the Friday night football game, you're feeding that dopamine rush as you anticipate the praise you'll receive.

Here's where the plot thickens, though. The more you say "yes," the more you train your brain to associate it with feeling good. And the guilt that comes with saying "no"? Oh, that guilt has a scientific basis too. According to neuroscientists, our brains are hardwired to avoid conflict. So, when we *don't* say "yes," we trigger the same stress response we feel when we think we're in danger. Yup, that's right—telling someone "no" can actually make your brain feel like it's in fight-or-flight mode. No wonder we all hate doing it!

And saying "yes" all the time isn't just bad for your mental health; it's physically draining too. Studies show that chronic overcommitment leads to higher levels of stress, fatigue, and even burnout. So while everyone else is chilling, you're out here running around like a headless chicken, wondering why you feel exhausted *all the time*.

And let's talk about guilt for a second. Guilt has this sneaky way of making you feel responsible for everyone else's happiness, when really, you're just out here overextending yourself. The *Guilt-Trip Express* is one-way only, and it's heading straight to the Land of Resentment.

Trust me, I remember my early years as a teacher—single, no kids, full of passion for the job and convinced my students *were* my kids. I was always the first one everyone asked to help with after-school activities or weekend events. And I said "yes." Every time. Those yeses made me feel like I belonged, like I was pulling my weight on the team. But after a year of never having a weekend to myself, the guilt that had originally driven me to say "yes" turned into resentment. I started resenting my coworkers for always volunteering me—and worse, I resented myself for not having the courage to say "no." Somewhere along the way, "the easy answer" became a burden.

There are also many social reasons that educators find themselves often saying "yes." As teachers, we often find ourselves taking part in a thankless competition to see who can juggle the most responsibilities. It's like a twisted game show where the prize is exhaustion! The more we say "yes," the more we feel the pressure to prove our worth as "dedicated" educators. But you don't need to pull a superhero act to validate your teaching abilities. Just showing up is already a win.

Remember that time you volunteered to lead a professional development workshop while your coffee cup was still half full? You were probably thinking, "If I don't do it, my principal will think I'm lazy" or "I can't let my colleagues down." News flash: Everyone is busy! While your enthusiasm is commendable, you are like a candle burning at both ends. The light may be bright, but the burnout will come quickly.

Then there's the lurking beast called *FOMO*, *fear of missing out*. When we say "no," we fear that we will miss out on a valuable experience. If you say "no" to that extra committee or after-school activity, will you miss out on networking opportunities? Will you miss the chance to bond with coworkers over snacks? Will you miss being in a photo posted on social media? Just because everyone else can take part in additional duties doesn't mean you have to. Instead of thinking of what you could miss if you don't take on additional tasks, focus on what you will gain by shifting your priorities. Could you gain extra time with your family? Would you gain an extra hour to go to the gym? Would you finally get to bed on time? You have to protect your own peace, my friend.

So what's the solution to overcommitment? Saying "no," and saying it with your chest. We previously discussed the importance of setting boundaries and communicating them. Getting comfortable with saying "no" helps you stick to your word. And baby, you gotta stick to your word like your mental health depends on it—because it actually does.

When you say "no," you're retraining your brain. You're telling it, "Hey, it's okay to prioritize myself. It's okay to let someone else carry the load." And guess what happens to that looming guilt? It starts to fade. Your brain learns that self-care isn't selfish, it's survival.

And the benefits go beyond just you. When teachers model healthy boundaries, students learn that it's okay to prioritize self-respect over people-pleasing. Schools begin to function more fairly because the "yes" isn't always falling on the same few shoulders. Communities grow stronger when everyone contributes from a place of genuine willingness rather than from one of burnout or obligation.

Saying "no" creates space. Space for rest. Space for joy. Space to say "yes" to the things that align with your values and vision.

Your brain loves dopamine, but it loves balance even more. So next time you feel that guilt creeping in, remember that saying "no" isn't shutting the door on compassion. It's opening the door to self-preservation.

The Domino Effect of Overcommitment

Let's dive in to the emotional and professional fallout of overcommitment. If you feel like you're drowning in responsibilities, it's high time for a reality check.

- **Emotional Exhaustion**: The first victim of overcommitment is your emotional well-being. You'll start feeling overwhelmed, stressed, and dare I say it, a little resentful. That initial joy you felt from teaching? It gets buried under a pile of "must-dos" and "should-haves."
- **Professional Burnout**: Burnout isn't just a trendy word; it's a sad reality for many educators. Studies show that overcommitment leads to burnout. When you take on more than you can reasonably handle, your job satisfaction and performance take a nosedive, and you may even start contemplating a career change. No teacher wants to end up googling "How to become a barista" after all the work they put into their career.
- **Impact on Your Students**: When you're stretched too thin, your students are the ones who suffer. An exhausted teacher means less energy and engagement in the classroom. If you're busy juggling meetings and responsibilities, you might miss that one student who really needs your attention.

Practical Techniques for Saying "No" Confidently

All right, enough of the doom and gloom. Let's talk about how to say "no" without feeling like you just committed a social faux pas. Saying "no" well involves clarity, kindness, and confidence. Start with a warm demeanor—smile gently, maintain calm eye contact, and keep your tone friendly but firm. Express gratitude first, state your boundary clearly, then close with openness if appropriate. This "gratitude–boundary–possibility" pattern helps protect your limits while preserving relationships and professionalism. In that light, here are some practical techniques for saying "no" that will help you feel empowered while keeping your dignity intact.

1. Understand Your Priorities

Before you can confidently wield the power of "no," you need to know what matters most to you. Is it family time? Your mental health? A clean house? Once you identify your top priorities, saying "no" becomes much easier.

Think of setting priorities like Tetris: you can only stack the blocks—your commitments—in a way that allows you to fit everything in without losing your mind. What are the most important blocks in your life? Focus on those and let the less important ones tumble away.

2. Practice the Art of the Polite Decline

Let's face it, nobody wants to come off as the villain at their school. You can be both polite and firm in saying "no" without feeling like you've just insulted someone's mom.

Here's a go-to script for when someone asks you to take on an extra duty: "Thanks so much for thinking of me! I'm truly flattered you want me involved, but I have to focus on my current commitments right now. Maybe next time!"

Boom! Friendly, respectful, and to the point. Translation: I'm booked and busy, but I still like you. And that "Maybe next time!" at the end? It's your exit strategy that keeps the vibes intact. This response affirms the relationship through gratitude and validation while confidently asserting a personal boundary without guilt or overexplaining. It also keeps the door open, leaving room for future collaboration without committing prematurely.

3. Use "I" Statements

When you say "no," center the conversation around your own needs. This shift helps eliminate the guilt you might feel about denying someone else's request.

Try saying something like: "I appreciate you asking, but I need to prioritize my time for my family right now. I hope you understand!"

Using "I" statements is a low-key power move. It keeps the focus on your experience without blaming or deflecting, which helps keep the conversation chill and nondefensive. Saying something like, "I need to prioritize rest tonight" centers your own boundaries instead of making it about someone else's request. It's a subtle but firm way to remind folks—without even saying it—that your time and energy aren't unlimited, and they deserve the same respect as anyone else's. It's respectful, clear, and grounded in self-awareness, which makes it easier for people to receive your "no."

4. Acknowledge the Request, Then Decline

If you want to soften the blow of your "no," acknowledge the request before you decline. This shows respect for the person's need while still drawing your line in the sand.

For instance: "I understand this is important, and I truly appreciate you thinking of me. However, I must decline this time as I'm currently committed to other projects."

Validation meets boundary setting is the ultimate win-win—it's like giving the other person a high five *before* you gently close the door. When you validate someone's request (e.g., "That sounds like an amazing project") you're showing that you respect their need, their effort, or their trust in you. It's the spoonful of sugar that helps the "no" go down easier. When people feel heard and appreciated, they are more likely to accept your boundary.

5. Leave Room for Future Involvement

Saying "no" doesn't mean you're severing ties forever. Let the person know you're still interested in future opportunities. This shows you're engaged but managing your current workload.

Try something like: "I can't take this on right now, but I'd love to be considered for future opportunities!"

It's like saying, "Not today, but maybe tomorrow!"—a gentle way of keeping the connection alive without sacrificing your current peace or priorities. This method works because it allows you to say "no" without burning bridges; you're not rejecting the person or their idea outright, you're just honoring your bandwidth in the moment. It gives you breathing room while reassuring the other person that you're open to collaboration in the future, on your terms. By leaving the door open, you maintain goodwill and flexibility, which can be especially helpful in work or personal relationships where you may want to say "yes" later.

6. Have a "No" Plan in Place

It's one thing to say "no," but how do you handle the inevitable follow-up? Be ready for the pushback. People might want an explanation, or they might try to sweet-talk you into saying "yes." Have your response ready!

Decide on your reasons ahead of time and practice how you'll respond. A simple line could be: "I'm currently balancing my commitments and need to prioritize my existing responsibilities. I hope you understand."

Having a "no" plan in place—complete with a Plan A and a backup Plan B—is essential, especially when you're dealing with leadership that's laser-focused on achieving their goals, sometimes by any means necessary. They're not being malicious; they're just driven. And if you're not ready, you might find yourself saying "yes" the second time around. Plan A might be your graceful, default decline: "Thanks for thinking of me, but I'm already committed to X right now." Plan B kicks in when the pressure rises—like when they ask again or sweeten the deal—and sounds like, "I appreciate the offer, but even with modifications, I still need to sit this one out."

Having these responses ready protects you from being caught off guard and helps you hold your boundaries. Because let's be honest, if you're not prepared to protect your time, someone else is already making plans for it.

7. Give Yourself Permission to Prioritize Yourself

Last but not least, remember that it's perfectly okay to put your needs first. Saying "no" isn't selfish; it's self-care. You're a human being with a life outside of the classroom, and it's crucial to protect your time and energy.

Sample Scripts and Situations

Now, let's roll up our sleeves and get practical. Here are some example scripts for the most common situations where you might need say "no."

- **Declining Extra Duties:** When a colleague asks you to take on another responsibility that you can't fit into your jam-packed schedule: "Thanks so much for considering me for this, but I need to decline. My schedule is pretty packed right now, and I want to make sure I can give my best to my current responsibilities."
- **Turning Down Unnecessary Meetings:** If your principal invites you to yet another meeting that you know will be a snooze-fest, say: "I appreciate the invite. However, I have some pressing matters to attend to that day. I trust I can catch up on any important notes afterward."
- **Refusing a Committee Position:** When you're asked to join another committee and your heart says, "nope," say: "I'm honored to be considered for this committee. However, I'm currently involved in several initiatives and won't be able to give it the attention it deserves. I hope you understand."
- **Saying "No" to Parent Requests:** If a parent requests a meeting outside of school hours, and you just can't swing it, say: "I appreciate your desire to discuss this. However, I'm unable to meet outside of school hours. I'm happy to connect during office hours or over email."
- **Declining an Invitation to an Event:** When you're invited to an after-school event but need some time to recharge, say: "Thank you for inviting me! I'd love to support, but I have prior commitments that evening. I hope it goes well!"

Embracing Your Right to Say "No"

At the end of the day, remember that saying "no" isn't a personal affront to anyone. It's a declaration of your right to prioritize your own needs. Saying "no" opens up space for you to say "yes" to the things that truly matter in your life and work.

You have the power to take a step back, breathe, and reclaim your time. The world won't implode because you chose not to take on every extra duty or responsibility. In fact, you might just find that when you give yourself the freedom to focus on what truly matters, you become a better teacher—not just for your students, but also for yourself.

So the next time someone approaches you with that familiar request for an extra favor, channel your inner queen (or king!) and don your armor of self-respect. You've got the right to protect your mental space and emotional bandwidth. Remember: You're not just a teacher; you're a human being with needs, aspirations, and a life outside of the classroom.

The Takeaways

Saying "yes" all the time is like adding weights to your backpack on a hike—at first you think you can handle it, but eventually, it slows you down and wears you out. As you continue this journey, remember these tips:

Know Your Worth

- Your value as an educator isn't measured by how many committees you serve on or how many extra duties you take on. Being a good teacher is ultimately about the quality of the connections you build with your students and the impact you make on their lives.

Practice Makes Perfect

- Like any new skill, saying "no" takes practice. Start small and work your way up to the bigger requests. You'll find that each "no" becomes easier with time.

Surround Yourself with Support

- Connect with colleagues who understand your journey and can offer you support. They may even inspire you to stand firm in your decision making.

Self-Care is Not Optional

- It's not selfish to prioritize yourself, it's essential! When you take care of your well-being, you're in a better position to care for your students and contribute meaningfully to your school community.

Reframe Your Mindset

- Shift your perspective from guilt to empowerment. Instead of thinking, "I'm letting someone down" when you say "no," remind yourself, "I'm honoring my boundaries and preserving my energy."

Now go out there and practice your "no." Own it! And when someone asks why you're saying "no," just smile and wave. Because at the end of the day, saying "no" is about embracing the right to choose what fills your heart and fuels your passion.

Chapter 3

THE ZEN WITHIN

See, What Had Happened Was: I Found Peace

Ever wanted to run away from your job, family, and anything associated with responsibility? That was me a while ago. I dreamt of having what I called a "me-cation" so I could reset with only the company of me, myself, and I. Somewhere between the never-ending chaos of life, I never made it happen. Plus, if I'm honest, I was kind of scared to plan an excursion. Not scared like "Somebody's gonna snatch me up," but more like, "Will this solo trip be worth it?"

Back then, life felt like a never-ending relay race—except I was almost every runner on the team. I was a teacher by day and partially still a teacher by night. After school I'd come home, switch gears, and cook dinner. Lesson planning or grading papers while watching television with the family was normal. My son had a social calendar that rivaled a small celebrity's: T-ball, soccer, playdates, birthday parties. And I was married, but let's be honest, I had little to no energy left for romance. Sunday was the only day I could breathe and let an hour of church do its healing while I side-eyed the clock, knowing Monday was already peeking around the corner.

Fast forward to almost a decade later, I was fresh out of a soul-snatching divorce that left me emotionally drained, I was trying to help my son navigate the wild world of high school while also figuring out how to adult solo—like, who knew houses needed this much maintenance? On top of that, I had just started a new job, so I was trying not to look like I was unraveling. I was exhausted—mentally, emotionally, spiritually—and I couldn't even hear myself think, let alone remember who I was outside of everybody else's needs. My life came tumbling down as the school year ended. You know how that last week is: classroom parties, packing up the room, preparing report cards, and making Honors Day run like the Grammys. And that was just my day job.

By the end of the school year, I was drained. I fell into bed one night, my energy tank completely empty. I wanted to pray for help, but I only mustered up enough energy to mouth, "I surrender." Right as I drifted off, I got a random text from a church I'd visited once. Just a generic invite to Sunday service, but for some reason, I couldn't shake it. Did my two-word prayer reach Heaven?

I went to church the next morning, and the whole sermon was about the importance of isolation. Y'all, I couldn't believe it. The pastor preached about the beauty of taking time alone, using everything from Moses to Elijah as examples of how isolation leads to clarity. I took this as a sign to retreat. I had no idea where I was going, but I knew I had to plan a weekend of solitude.

That same day a friend I hadn't talked to in years called me out of the blue. I told her about my desire for a much-needed vacation. "Well, I'm going to be out of town for a month, and you're welcome to stay at my place in California," she casually replied. A whole house, for free, for nearly a month! The cherry on top was my son's summer camp occurring the exact same month.

And just like that, the stars aligned. I had a location and lodging for my me-cation. Then the universe said, "Wait, sis, we're not done." I received an invitation to a casino-themed party and accepted, fully expecting to just learn how to play blackjack while sipping on cocktails. Next thing I know, the host is like, "It's raffle time!" and boom—my ticket gets pulled. And not for a bottle of wine or a cheesy parting gift. Honey, I won a whole $1,000 Visa gift card. I legit hit the jackpot . . . flight money *and* spending cash secured. It was like the universe handed me a trip on a silver platter. Blessings on blessings!

Y'all, the trip was fabulous. The house was ten minutes from the beach, forty minutes from LA, and I had a whole month to myself. I walked and biked daily, soaking up the sunshine and salty air. I even shifted my diet, cooking fresh meals most nights then trying trendy vegetarian spots in between. The time and space helped me clear my mind and be present in the moment. It was then that I realized peace wasn't something I had to chase. It was already within me.

The extrovert in me led me to new friends. I attended yoga classes, had drinks with a guy I met at the beach, and even hit up a comedy show with a few locals. But the core of that trip was about me—finding my calm, my balance. My me-cation was straight out of a Julia Roberts *Eat, Pray, Love* scene. I came back refreshed, more emotionally grounded, and finally tuned in to myself in a way that felt brand new.

This was Zen. Traditionally, Zen is a form of Buddhism focused on meditation, mindfulness, and direct experience over religious doctrine. For me, Zen has more of a secular vibe—staying steady and keeping my cool without needing a retreat in the mountains. It's about creating pockets of peace in the middle of the madness and choosing calm like it's part of my everyday outfit.

On this trip Zen was about self-realization—getting in touch with what my soul needed. I wasn't thinking about work or family obligations. I was just in the moment, letting go of stress and fully embracing the present.

So what does my me-cation have to do with your teacher lifestyle? Chile, everything! The trip wasn't about running away from my life, as I'd first envisioned it. It was about checking in with myself. It was about clearing my mind, finding balance, and doing what feeds my soul.

In the end, no one died because I was away for a month. My house was still intact when I returned, and my son actually enjoyed the break from me. And I came back better—a whole new asset to myself, my family, and the world around me. And the best part? I learned that it's okay to check out and feed your soul, guilt-free.

We all need the attitude and perspective I gained from my me-cation as we continue in this profession. We need to carry an inner calm. We need clarity to think and tackle tough problems. And we need moments for ourselves. So let's learn how to channel this calm as we navigate the world of education, shall we?

What Does It Mean to Find Zen?

Okay, before we get started, I must address a few of our teacher friends who just sighed, thinking, "Girl, how can I even think about Zen when I've got stacks of ungraded papers and zero planning time?" Trust me, I get it. Been there, done that, got the T-shirt.

When I say "find Zen," I don't mean you have to walk around in flowing robes, speak in riddles, and have students sit in a lotus position all day (although if you can pull that off, you are Teacher of the Century). Being a Zen teacher is all about finding calm in the middle of all the chaos—being the eye of the storm while everything else is spinning around you. It's about not letting the constant stream of demands, distractions, and downright craziness steal your peace.

I didn't come to Zen through a temple or a silent retreat. I found it through author Jay Shetty, who made ancient wisdom feel like it belonged in my everyday life. His teachings, like, "You can't be everything to everyone and still be something to yourself," and "When you learn to navigate the noise, you can hear your own voice," helped me understand that Zen isn't about escaping life; it's about learning how to live it with presence. He talks a lot about intention, stillness, and purpose—how your morning routine can shape your mind-set, how gratitude grounds you, and how "the biggest room in the world is the room for self-improvement." Through Jay's lens, Zen became a mind-set for me: choosing calm in chaos, clarity over clutter, and inner peace as a daily practice, not a once-a-year vacation.

Let me give you a visual: Picture yourself as that one chill person at the airport when everyone else is losing their minds because their flight's delayed. Imagine that you're that one person calmly sipping your overpriced coffee, reading a book, while chaos unfolds around you. You're not stressing—you're just vibing, knowing the flight will take off when it takes off. That's you when you are in your Zen.

Stress is not something you can banish entirely from your life. You are a teacher, after all. But you can choose how you react to it. That's where the Zen mind-set comes in. Zen is not about pretending everything is perfect; it's about learning to breathe, center yourself, and keep it moving even when the world is on fire.

Many of you probably think Zen is just all fluff. Some of you might think it's too spiritual, too unrealistic, or just not made for people who are juggling real-life responsibilities. And for a lot of teachers especially, the idea of adding one more thing to an already-packed day feels exhausting. The skepticism is real, and I don't blame anyone for feeling that way. After all, Zen has been wrapped in mystery and aesthetics for years for many of us, making it feel out of reach.

Zen, at its core, isn't about perfection or pretending life is calm when it's not. It's about awareness, about learning to pause before reacting, and protecting your mental and emotional space. You don't need a meditation cushion or a spiritual guru. You just need a moment of quiet in your car before walking into the building, a deep breath before responding to that parent email, or the decision to say "no" to one more after-school obligation. Zen isn't a task; it's a shift in how you carry the ones you already have.

So yes, being a Zen teacher is possible—especially for those of you who feel like you don't have time for Zen. You don't have to overhaul your life or pretend you're above frustration. You just have to choose peace, on purpose, a little more often.

Maintaining Calm in the Classroom

Being a Zen teacher ultimately boils down to cultivating a strong sense of acceptance. You know those moments when you feel like everything is happening at once? One kid just spilled their juice, another forgot their homework, and you just received three emails from admin asking for something that was due yesterday right now? Yeah, those moments are prime time to unleash your Zen superpowers and find calm in the storm. But how can you keep your cool when the world's on fire?

Strategy 1: Embrace the Art of Pausing

First up, let's stop trying to fix everything immediately. Who told us we have to be superheroes, handling every issue the second it pops up? Take it from me, you don't need to be on top of *everything* all the time. You're allowed to take a breath. You don't have to fix every problem or respond to every email in the next five seconds.

When the day starts spinning out of control—students asking a million questions, technology malfunctioning, emails piling up—take a second to just *pause*. When things get wild, pause and *breathe*. Trust me, the classroom isn't going to implode in the thirty seconds it takes you to collect yourself.

Teaching your students that they don't have to have the answers to everything immediately will help them develop problem-solving skills *and* keep their stress levels down, so it's important to get them on the same wavelength. After all, Zen is all about helping your students to find their calm too. Encourage them to take a moment before jumping into a solution. Try incorporating a daily mindfulness practice, like a one-minute breathing exercise at the start or end of class. Finding a break with your students could be as simple as saying, "Before we dive in, let's all take a deep breath and reset."

Better yet, create spaces in your classroom that encourage reflection. Designate a "chill corner"—whether it's a spot to doodle, read, or just sit quietly—where students can step away for a few minutes if they're feeling overwhelmed. This kind of environment fosters emotional regulation and helps students learn that sometimes hitting pause is the best move.

Strategy 2: Own Your Space

Part of staying Zen is owning the energy of your classroom. If you're calm, you'll help your students calm down too (or at least make them question why they're experiencing big emotions). Cultivating calm in the classroom doesn't mean you have to go all monotone and emotionless (Nobody's asking you to be a robot). But set the vibe you want by choosing your own energy first. If you come in calm and grounded, you'll be surprised by how much control you actually have over the room. Start the day with calm energy, and it'll ripple through your classroom like a chill wave.

I had this seventh-grade boy once who was basically a walking bundle of anxiety. Every single day, he would rush into my room, on edge, running up to me with frantic updates about how he left his book in his locker or did the wrong homework, his hands trembling as he talked. You could feel the stress radiating off of him like a heater. I knew I had to step in, not just for his sake, but for the energy of the whole class.

So I worked with him one-on-one. But even more than that, I had a strict class rule: "positive vibes only." It wasn't just a cute phrase—I really meant it. My classroom had to be a place where negativity, anxiety, and stress hit a wall. I created this invisible barrier of love—self-love and love for my students—and the anxious energy stopped at the door.

It didn't take long for him to recognize that our space invited calm, and he naturally adjusted his energy to match.

I aimed to offer this student calmness and consistency, knowing that grounding his anxiety with steadiness—not feeding into it—was the most effective way to support him. I taught this student that before he even spoke to me, he had to take a breath and check in with himself. He learned that most things weren't emergencies. And, little by little, he began to adjust. His hands stopped shaking, and he started coming into class more centered and more in control. When he did slip back into that anxious state, he knew how to calm down because the class vibe was all about growth and positivity.

If a student is bringing high-level anxiety into the room, set the tone early on. Create an environment where they know the expectation is to reset and focus on solutions, not panic. Help them to see that mistakes aren't the end of the world, and model how to breathe through difficult moments. Once your student realizes you're not buying into their anxiety, they'll start letting go of it too.

This method worked wonders with my anxious student. I remember the day he confidently walked into class, no rush, no panic, just a "Good morning, Dr. Ledford!" He had forgotten his book (again), but instead of spiraling, he calmly asked, "May I go get it after we start?" This was growth. And the best part? He taught himself how to carry that energy beyond my classroom.

Strategy 3: Don't Take It Personally

While we may lead our classrooms, it's nevertheless important that we don't take chaos personally. Yes, that kid who just knocked over the globe and threw their pencil at the ceiling is being annoying. But their energy doesn't have to mess with yours.

The idea that we need to take our egos out of our classroom crises may be difficult to absorb. Before I go on, then, please know I certainly do not mean for you to ignore behaviors that need to be addressed.

If your classroom looks like a playground at recess, there's a great chance you need to incorporate some new behavior-management tactics. But it's also important to remember that the chaos is rarely about *you* personally.

Most student behavior stems from unmet needs, developmental stages, outside stressors, or simply a lack of clear boundaries—not from some targeted mission to disrupt your peace. When we can separate our identity from the behavior in front of us, we make room for clarity, strategy, and compassion instead of taking every disruption as a personal failure.

I used to get so wrapped up in the daily antics of my classroom. Like, why are my students doing this to me?! The thing is they aren't ever doing anything *to me*; they're just being themselves, and sometimes they're a hot mess. Behavior issues are not about you, and it's not your job to control everything in your classroom. Repeat after me: "Not. My. Circus."

If you read that and mumbled, "It *is* my circus," I totally understand. It *is* your classroom, and in many ways, you *are* the ringmaster. But here's where it gets more nuanced: While you're responsible for creating the structure, tone, and expectations of your space, the emotional chaos students bring in isn't always yours to fix or absorb. Yes, you're leading the show, but not every act in the circus reflects your skills or failures. Some chaos is developmental, some is circumstantial, and some is simply out of your control. The key is learning to lead with intention, not ego, so you can respond to the mess with clarity instead of internalizing it as a personal attack.

I learned the importance of detachment the hard way when I taught a fourth grader whose mood swings could rival a summer thunderstorm—hot one minute, cold the next. He'd get mad over the smallest things, like a missing pencil or someone taking "his" chair, and then blow up. The yelling, the storming out, the defiance—it felt personal, especially because I was the one who was always rooting for him.

But as I got to know this student, I realized his story was heartbreaking. His dad was incarcerated for armed robbery, his brother was murdered in a gang-related incident, and his mom worked night shifts. This left him to care for himself and his little sister. He was a ten-year-old kid, but life had already handed him way more than he could handle. He was angry, not just at me, but at the world. And no matter how much love I poured into him, it couldn't undo the harm that had already taken root.

When this student yelled at me, fought with other kids at recess, or refused to do his work, I took it personally. I thought, "How could he treat me like this?" But the reality was, the student's rage wasn't about me. His anger was about a whole lot of things going on *outside* of school that I couldn't fix.

As much as we teachers like to call our students "our kids," they're not. We didn't birth them. They're not even a limb of our family tree. And they're navigating rules and philosophies on life that may completely differ from ours.

It took me a while to realize that no matter how much I cared or how hard I tried, I wasn't going to fix this student's life. I could only do my best to create a classroom where he felt safe and offer him as much consistency as I could. But I couldn't take his anger personally; it wasn't mine to carry.

Instead, I had to set my own boundaries. When my student blew up, I had to remind myself: "Not. My. Circus." His life, his struggles—they weren't a reflection of me or my ability to teach. I wasn't going to let his behavior derail the positive and productive systems I had worked so hard to create in the classroom.

To reframe a lesson from Chapter 1, you can love your students deeply and still set boundaries at the same time. With that in mind, I started making sure this student knew that while I was rooting for him, his behavior wasn't going to mess with our class's energy. I had to be the calm in his storm, and slowly, he began to trust that even when he was upset, I wasn't going anywhere.

So when the classroom starts to feel like a three-ring circus, remember to keep the peace, set your boundaries, and don't let anyone else's chaos steal your calm.

Practicing Mindfulness

Calm is great, but it isn't enough to get you through the day. Enter: Mindfulness. Sounds fancy, right? But mindfulness is real simple—it just means your brain is actually paying attention to what's happening right now. When you're mindful, you're focused on what you're doing, and you're tuned into the space you're in. Sounds basic, but let's be real—we don't always stay mindful.

Our minds? They're all over the place. One minute you're teaching, the next you're thinking about that awkward convo you had with your coworker or stressing over possible scenarios of an upcoming observation. And suddenly anxiety hits, and you're spiraling. But that's not what we're going for, is it? We're trying to *stay Zen.*

So let's dive into some super quick and easy mindfulness hacks you can sprinkle throughout your day to keep yourself grounded and your vibe intact.

Strategy 1: Breathing Exercises

The easiest (and most effective) mindfulness tool is literally right under your nose—your breath. Yep, that's it. When everything starts to feel like too much, and you're two seconds away from throwing in the towel, stop and *breathe.*

And no, I'm not talking about those quick, panicky, shallow breaths that feel like they're doing nothing but keeping you upright. I'm talking about deep belly breaths—the kind that hit your soul. In through your nose, out through your mouth, slow and steady. Do this a few times, and you'll begin to feel more relaxed.

It may be hard to know when you'd benefit from mindful breathing. So let's break down three perfect moments in your day where you can sneak in Zen-inducing breaths:

1. Morning routine: Before students enter the classroom, while you're sipping your coffee (or chugging it, no judgment), take a pause. Close your eyes, take a deep breath in through your nose, hold it for a second, then slowly release it. Inhale the calm, exhale any present (or even potential) negativity. I know it may sound silly, but honey, just five slow, intentional breaths can set the tone for the whole day.
2. Evening routine: This is the moment to treat yourself to that bubble bath. And yes, I said bubble bath! Because why are you spending all those Franklins on a spa day when you have hot water at home? If everyone else in the house can spend an hour in the bathroom, pretending to take care of business when they are really on their devices, you can take a guilt-free bath. Light some candles, play some music (just type "Zen music" into your music streaming app of choice), and just focus on your breathing. Trust me, you'll feel like you're floating by the time you're done.
3. Nightly ritual: Before you go to bed, you gotta put that cell phone down. Like all the way down. Otherwise, in five seconds you'll be down the rabbit hole watching videos of classroom transformations and dance trends. Instead of checking Instagram, take a moment to breathe deeply and let your whole body relax. If you're into prayer or meditation, this is the perfect time to combine them with mindful breathing. Exhale the worries of the day and inhale the calm you need for tomorrow. By the time you're done, you'll be so relaxed you might not even remember falling asleep.

Breathing is like your built-in reset button, and it's always there when you need it. So whether you're prepping for the day, winding down, or somewhere in between, those deep breaths can make all the difference.

Strategy 2: Breaks Are Your Best Friend

You know those five minutes you get between classes, or that moment you have before everyone realizes you are off from work? Yeah, those are sacred. Don't spend them answering emails or reorganizing your lesson plans for the five hundredth time. Take that time for you. Step outside, stretch, take a walk, drink some water—do something that makes you feel like a human being, not a teaching machine. Taking a break is like closing all of those open apps running in the background of your cell phone, draining the battery life. After you give yourself a moment, you can come back to class with fresh energy.

Taking a break doesn't need to take much time. Here are three quick ways to get that much-needed breather:

1. Get Outta Dodge: If there's no rule against leaving campus, do it! Seriously, my favorite thing to do during breaks is to walk around the area surrounding my school. If the neighborhood isn't safe, or the weather isn't great, I hop in my car and take a spin around the block. Just a change of scenery does wonders for your mind. Whether you're listening to your favorite playlist or tuned into a podcast, that little getaway can lift your spirits and give you a fresh perspective when you return.
2. Mindful Movement: Get up and move. Take a stroll around the school or do a few laps around the playground. Just the act of walking can clear your head and give you a boost of energy. As you take your break, try to be present in that moment—notice the trees, the sky, or even just the sound of your footsteps. It's amazing how a few minutes of movement can help reset your day and make you feel more grounded.

3. Car Therapy: When you get home, don't rush inside like you're trying to escape the storm. Park the car and just sit there for ten minutes. Seriously, soak in the silence. If you've got a dog or a kid that'll sniff you out, just park down the block for a hot minute. Trust me, they'll have no clue you're hiding out, and you can take those precious moments to breathe, reflect, or even scroll through social media without interruption.

When chaos starts to creep in, give yourself permission to step away, recharge, and come back ready to conquer whatever comes your way.

Strategy 3: Anchor Yourself in the Present

You know those moments when your mind starts spiraling into that endless to-do list or panicking about that parent email you haven't even opened yet? Yeah, we've all been there. When that happens, just stop. One of the best tricks I've picked up for staying mindful in the classroom is mastering the art of focusing right here, right now. Look around, notice what's happening, feel the floor under your feet, listen to the sounds in the room. Anchoring yourself in the present is a game changer for staying calm.

And here's where my secret weapon comes into play: music. When I need to keep it chill and steady, I play some neosoul, lo-fi, or cozy coffee shop tunes. Relaxing music is like an instant calming blanket for my brain.

But when the clock is ticking and I've got to crank out a mountain of work, I switch it up to some high-energy pop or rap. Time for some Tyler and Kendrick! Let me tell you, there's nothing like a fast beat to keep me from drifting into la-la land. I'm too busy humming or singing along to focus on anything else. It's a total game changer for staying grounded and present.

Creating Mental Space for Reflection

Reflection is a vital mindfulness tool because it creates space to slow down and understand what's happening beneath the surface. It shifts us from autopilot to intentional action, helping us notice patterns, celebrate growth, and realign with our purpose—especially when the day feels overwhelming. Reflection involves you creating mental space to *actually think*—to step back from the daily grind and reflect on what's working, what's not, and what you need.

Strategy 1: Carve Out Time for Reflection

First off, reflection isn't going to happen unless you make it happen; you've got to carve out precious time to sit with your thoughts and check in with yourself. Maybe you set aside a moment first thing in the morning, or maybe you make time at the end of the day when the classroom is finally quiet. Whatever works for you, make reflection time a habit.

Combine your moments of reflection with other calming habits, like deep breathing or that luxurious soak in the tub. Imagine this: You're settling into your bubble bath, the warm water enveloping you, and as you breathe in the soothing scents of your favorite bath oil, you allow your mind to wander and reflect. It's a two-for-one deal for your mental health!

As you reflect, ask yourself questions like:

- What made me feel grateful today?
- What challenged me, and how did I handle it?
- Did I take time for myself, and how can I make that a priority tomorrow?
- What moments brought me joy?
- How can I improve my energy for tomorrow?

You can't stay Zen if you never take the time to check in with how you're actually feeling, so get cozy and give yourself that well-deserved moment of peace.

Strategy 2: Use Reflection to Avoid Overwhelm

You know that feeling when you've got fifty things on your to-do list, and it all feels like too much? Yeah, reflection is your best tool for avoiding that feeling.

Back in college, my intern professor mandated daily journaling after work. I was all about the writing life, but journaling felt like one more chore on top of all of the lesson plans that had to be approved before I taught them. I was ready to hightail it out of that school and live my fabulous twenty-one-year-old life, not stay there another fifteen minutes just to write about my day.

At the time, I didn't realize that my professor was trying to instill in me the habit of reflection. She wanted me to take a breather and think about what went well that day, what I wanted to improve, or maybe just vent on those lined pages of a journal that no one would ever see. Journaling was like a combination of screaming into a pillow and having a chat with a therapist.

Take time each day to reflect on what's working and what's not. What's actually important for tomorrow, and what can wait? When you take a step back to reflect, you can start to see what's overwhelming you, and you can make a plan to deal with it before it takes over your life.

Strategy 3: Be Real with Yourself

Are you juggling too much? Clinging to stress like it's your new best friend? Let's face it, sometimes we can be our own worst enemy when it comes to managing stress because we're caught up in a relentless quest for perfection. True reflection is about keeping it real with yourself.

When you carve out time for reflection, you can genuinely evaluate how you're feeling. This practice helps you identify what you can let go of, where you might need some support, and how to move forward without burning out.

So that you don't go into autopilot, it's important to make reflection engaging—whether you're flying solo or teaming up with a buddy.

Solo Reflection Activities

1. **Reflective Walks:** Grab your earbuds and turn on your favorite music or just let the sounds of nature accompany you (my personal favorite). As you stroll, focus on your thoughts. What went well today? What could have been better? Let the fresh air cleanse your mind.
2. **Journaling:** Find a cozy spot at home or in a coffee shop and spill your thoughts onto the pages of your journal. Let your feelings flow, and don't hold back. It's your space, so make it work for you!

Partner Reflection Activities

1. **Sip and Share:** Taking a break with a trusted coworker can be both refreshing and productive. Whether it's over coffee, tea, or smoothies, "breaking bread" together gives you space to recharge, swap ideas, and support one another. Just remember: Without intention, the time can easily drift into gossip or distractions. Try setting a light agenda, keep the focus educational, and you'll walk away feeling both relaxed and inspired. Save the alcoholic beverages for a more casual event.
2. **Wine Down Wednesdays:** Turn those midweek blues into a reflective session with a friend! I know you're inclined to wait till the weekend, but just know that a hump day break may be what you need to keep you going. Plus, reflecting with a

friend can keep your thoughts separate from the workplace. Share what's been weighing you down while sipping on some wine or a mocktail. Just be sure to keep it focused—reflection first, bubbly and gossip later!

3. **FaceTime & Feedback:** You don't need to be in the same room to feel supported. Schedule a quick FaceTime or video chat with a friend or fellow educator. Keep it simple and intentional—each person shares one win, one challenge, and one goal for the week. Having someone listen and respond with encouragement (or honest perspective) can shift your mindset in ten to fifteen minutes flat.
4. **Walk Together + Reflect:** Sometimes movement helps make space for mental clarity. Invite a friend, partner, or fellow educator to take a walk with you (after school, during a prep, or even on the weekend). Use the time to reflect aloud: What's bringing you joy? What's draining you? What's one thing you want to do differently next week? Plus, nature and fresh air can give you the kind of perspective that four classroom walls just can't.

Whether you spend time reflecting alone or with a trusted partner, just remember to keep it real. Reflection is your time to shine a light on what's happening inside and how you can cultivate a healthier mindset.

The Takeaways

Listen, no one's saying you're going to walk into your classroom tomorrow and suddenly be a Zen master. But if you can, start practicing some of these strategies:

Tap into Your Zen Mode

- Embrace a new mindset where teaching doesn't have to mean chaos and exhaustion. Being a "Zen mode" teacher is all about staying calm, focused, and centered—even when the copier jams or the Wi-Fi is down.

Keep a Calm Classroom

- Create a peaceful atmosphere for yourself and your students. Use intentional techniques like speaking calmly, simplifying your routines, and setting boundaries to keep the stress out and the good vibes in.

Mindfulness Moments

- Find time to pause and breathe. Use quick mindfulness tricks like deep breathing exercises, taking a quiet moment between classes, or stepping outside for fresh air. Small breaks can make a big difference in your mental state.

Finding Zen is all about progress, not perfection. The key is to find your own path to calm in the middle of the teaching storm. And if that means taking an extra five minutes to breathe or just giving yourself permission to not have it all together, do it. You deserve to feel at peace in your classroom.

Now excuse me while I go outside for a breath of fresh air.

Part 2

BUILDING SUSTAINABLE WORK HABITS

Chapter 4

RECLAIMING YOUR TIME

See, What Had Happened Was: We Changed Fall Festival

At a school where I once taught, shortly after school kicked off, we would get hit with the first real signs of autumn—the cool breezes, the leaves showing off their new colors, and *drumroll please* . . . the Fall Festival. It's different at every school, but it all boils down to candy, hayrides, and that one mom who treats the bake sale like she's a contestant on *Nailed It!*

Teachers are manning face paint stations and bouncy houses. Principals are taking shifts in the dunk tank. Somewhere in the gym, the DJ has gotten half of the crowd to do the electric slide like it's a family reunion. The night is all about building community, raising funds, and having fun. For one night it's less about grades and more about glow sticks, giggles, and getting down on the dance floor.

Sure, the Fall Festival is *fun* in theory—kids laughing, parents mingling, and money rolling in for much-needed classroom supplies. But can we talk about the downside? After a week of teaching, the *last* thing

I have ever wanted to do on a Friday evening is to collect tickets, play DJ for musical chairs, or babysit the line for the bouncy house.

Sometimes the event organizers would even have the audacity to ask me if I wanted to volunteer for the dunk tank. Ruin my silk-pressed bob and catch pneumonia? Absolutely not. What I really need to kick off the weekend at the start of the new school year is to be at a bar, sipping a margarita and dipping chips into guac. Instead, my semester essentially began with the Fall Festival for many years.

One fall, though, one of the teachers—bless her innovative soul—convinced the principal to host the Fall Festival *during* school hours. Yes, you read that right—*during the day.* The festival still had all the bells and whistles. From hayrides to face painting, students had the opportunity to run themselves ragged with their friends. But instead of us teachers clocking in overtime, parents and volunteers showed up to set up and run the stations. We had a rotating schedule where grade levels brought their students to the festivities in blocks, and when the time was up, we went back to class like normal. The kids had a blast, the school raised its money, and I was in my car on my way to my much-needed margarita on time (hair intact).

When that teacher made her innovative suggestion, it was like someone opened a window in a stuffy room. Sure, her innovativeness saved the day, but there is a broader takeaway. Sometimes we're so used to overfunctioning that we forget we're allowed to question the "way it's always been." What made the solution feel impossible wasn't the logistics—it was the silent culture of burnout, where teachers assumed exhaustion was just part of the job, not a fixable problem. All it took to reclaim our time was a little out-of-the-box thinking while staying *well* within the boundaries.

Between meetings that could've been emails, grading homework that half of the kids rush through anyway, and impromptu after-school conferences with parents who want to know why Johnny can't multiply by eight, a teacher's time slips away faster than your motivation on a Monday morning.

But we're not here to dwell on the impossible. Nah, this chapter is all about reclaiming your time like you're Maxine Waters in the middle of a congressional meeting. Because, believe it or not, you *can* take back control of your life, and it starts with cutting out the nonsense.

Identifying the Time-Wasters

While my Fall Festival story reveals a time when my time *was* reclaimed, an event like that only happens once a year and won't heavily impact your whole year. In fact, most of your time-drains aren't tied to mandated events; they're often the result of our own choices and lack of intentional time management.

As educators, we're acutely aware that there are only twenty-four hours in a day, yet we often act as if those hours are limitless, as if we can hit a magical rewind button and retrieve the hours we've lost. This illusion of abundance leads us to overcommit, overextend, and overlook opportunities to protect our most valuable resource—our time.

So let's talk about the energy suckers that live rent-free in your day. We've all got them. They lurk in the corners of your lesson-planning sessions and pop up during your only free period like, "Hey, can you just . . . ?" Time-wasters are the *frenemies* of your professional life—dressed up as "important tasks," but secretly stealing your sanity one minute at a time.

Pointless Meetings

Let's start with the obvious villain: pointless meetings. You know the ones I'm talking about. They have no real agenda, they drag on longer than a student's excuse for not doing their homework, and they leave you wondering how an hour of your life just vanished. These meetings are like gathering all of your neighbors together to discuss whether painting your mailbox breaks the HOA rules.

Solution: Unless the meeting is crucial to your day or involves something that directly impacts you or your classroom, don't be afraid to ask for the CliffsNotes version. "Can you just send that in an email?" might sound like a dream phrase, but trust me, it's your new mantra. And when you're leading a meeting? Be sure it's like a good espresso shot—short, strong, and gets the job done without dragging things out.

Pleasant Interruptions

Then there's always that one colleague who rolls up to your room like you're running a therapy session or hosting a morning talk show. You're at your desk, deep in grading mode, hustling to finish before the next class, and in walks Chatty Cathy, ready to unload all the details of her weekend, her boyfriend drama, or whatever's been floating around in her head. And it's not that you don't like Cathy. She's cool. Your schedule is just already so tight you can barely fit in your work obligations.

Solution: Listen, I love a good catch-up, but there's a time and place. If you've got stuff to do, politely redirect the conversation. Try this line: "Girl, I'm dying to hear all about it, but I'm swamped right now. Can we catch up during lunch?" Keep it light, keep it polite, but most importantly, keep it moving.

Surprise Assignments

As teachers, we're never at a loss for things to do. You know how someone just *magically* adds things to your plate, and it's never clear how it happened? Like, you blink, and suddenly you're responsible for organizing the talent show, the science fair, and the annual pancake breakfast. When did we agree to this?

And don't even get me started on how everyone assumes you'll automatically take over whatever the last person in your role was passionate about. You become department chair, and suddenly you're expected to run Tammy's annual breast cancer rally because she did it for the last ten years. Tammy's mom had breast cancer, which is why she cared so deeply. But you? You just wanted to wear pink and donate your money. Now you're stuck in meetings creating fundraising goals and searching for a vendor who will supply a bulk of pink ribbons.

Solution: Look, just because someone suggests you'd be great at something doesn't mean you're automatically signed up for it. Practice saying "no"—remember, we already covered this in the last chapter, so you've got this! Don't let those phantom assignments sneak their way onto your plate. If it's not part of your job description or something you're truly passionate about, feel free to sidestep it with grace. You're not a human backpack carrying every school event.

Better yet, take a moment to reflect on what you care about. What's your passion? How can you bring that to your role in a way that doesn't require after-hours meetings and weekend events? Who says everything has to happen after school anyway?

Get creative and incorporate your ideas into the regular school day. Want to host a book club? Make it a recess activity. Got a community service project in mind? Build it into class time. Not every great idea has to take place after 3 p.m. when you're already running on fumes. Set those boundaries, and if you do take something on, make it work for you.

Creating a Time-Management System That Prioritizes You

While it's important to identify and avoid time-wasters, reclaiming your time is also a matter of *making* time for what matters—and optimizing your schedule accordingly. The goal is to organize your day so that you actually have time for yourself. I know—revolutionary concept, right?

Strategy 1: The Prioritization Matrix

A prioritization matrix can be a fantastic way to tame an unruly schedule. Don't freak out because this sounds fancier than it really is. Basically you need to figure out what's urgent, what's important, and what can be put on the back burner. Imagine you're a music producer who is tasked with putting together a Destiny's Child reunion concert. You have to decide which tasks are your headliners and which ones are just background singers.

The Matrix Breakdown:

- Urgent and Important: These are the Beyoncés of your day. They are the star tasks that demand all your attention. You've got to handle them now. Think grading those final exams that are due tomorrow, prepping for that observation lesson your principal is sitting in on, or submitting report card grades before the system locks you out.
- Important but Not Urgent: These are the Kelly Rowlands of your list. Still crucial, still slaying, but they can wait until you've handled Queen Bey. These are things like writing feedback for student projects, updating your curriculum plan for next semester, or attending a committee meeting that's two weeks away.
- Urgent but Not Important: Ah, the Michelle Williams of your to-dos—things like refilling the color ink in the copier or adding a screw to your "thinking chair" that's been moved to the corner. They definitely create harmony in our classrooms, but the show can go on without them. Delegate these tasks when you can.
- Not Urgent or Important: The LaTavias. We love them, but if you let them fall off the radar, much of the world will never know. This goes for stuff like organizing your desk drawers,

filing paperwork from six months ago, or attending that optional meeting about a club you're not even involved in.

Once you've started tackling the things that move the needle, delegating tasks, and letting go of any busywork, you begin to have a clear roadmap for action. The point isn't to do everything faster; it's to do the right things with more clarity and less stress.

The real power of the prioritization matrix is how it shifts your mindset. Instead of constantly reacting to whatever's loudest or most stressful, you're making intentional choices about how to spend your time. You're not meant to do everything—you're meant to do what matters most. This tool gives you permission to stop glorifying busyness and start clearing space for what actually deserves your attention.

Strategy 2: Time Blocking

If you constantly feel like you're running on a hamster wheel, then time blocking is especially important for you. The technique is simple: block out chunks of time on your calendar for specific tasks and stick to it.

Here's how it works:

- **Morning Block**: Use this for your high-energy tasks—lesson plans, important emails, and mandatory meetings that need your focus.
- **Midday Block**: Tackle medium-energy tasks here, like grading and updating the class newsletter.
- **Afternoon Block**: By now, you're probably running on fumes, so save this time for low-energy stuff like organizing your desk or prepping for the next day.

Time blocking can be highly beneficial because it allows you to allocate specific periods for important tasks, promotes focus, and reduces decision fatigue throughout the day. By visually organizing your schedule, you can manage your workload more effectively and ensure that high-priority tasks receive adequate attention. However, you gotta remember that because you work in a school and life be life-ing, time blocking has some limitations.

The rigid structure of time blocking may not always accommodate the unpredictable nature of a school environment. Like, you can have your whole day mapped out, feeling on top of the world, and then boom—a random fire drill, a pop-up meeting, or the god-forbidden Wi-Fi disconnection. Suddenly your whole schedule's doing backflips. If you don't leave a little room for flexibility, you're basically setting yourself up for chaos and coffee-fueled panic.

And guess what? Self-care is a block too. Yup, you're going to set aside time in your day to give your brain a break. And for those of you who normally work during your break: Stop it. You are not a robot. Give yourself a mental pause. Go eat. Go for a walk. Go sit in your car in silence or entertain yourself with Cathy's drama for a few minutes.

Strategy 3: The Two-Minute Rule

The two-minute rule is all about tackling procrastination. It helps cut through the mental clutter by making it easier to act on small tasks before they pile up into a mountain. If a task can be done in less than two minutes, just do it. Don't overthink it, don't put it on your to-do list—just get it done. This keeps you from wasting time on little things that tend to pile up like those student excuses about missed homework.

Why is the two-minute rule so amazing? Because sometimes our brains will procrastinate on the small stuff that piles up, which makes everything feel overwhelming later. By handling little things immediately, you're clearing mental clutter and keeping your to-do list from becoming the Mount Everest of stress.

Time-Management Tips for Teachers with ADHD

For many educators time management is overwhelming in and of itself. For those of us who are clinically diagnosed with attention deficit hyperactivity disorder (ADHD), organizing our schedules is like chasing glitter in the wind. Don't worry, though, because I've got you. There are some realistic, sanity-saving time-management tips that will help you boss up without burning out.

Strategy 1: Break It Down Like a TikTok Dance

If your tasks feel overwhelming, no worries. Treat your to-do list like learning choreography. You don't try to master the whole routine at once, right? Instead, chop tasks up into bite-sized moves. Instead of staring at a mountain of papers, grade a few at a time and take breaks in between until you're done. The dopamine hit from checking off minitasks is pure gold.

Example: You've got thirty essays to grade, but instead of grading all thirty in one sitting, do five during your planning period, five during lunch, and the rest after school. Place the work from your amazing writers in the beginning, middle, and end. Spread work out so your brain doesn't get bored and go rogue.

Strategy 2: Use Timers Like You're Speed Dating

Set a timer and commit to just ten or fifteen minutes of focused work. ADHD brains love a good sense of urgency! When the timer's up, take a quick break. If you're still in the groove, keep going, but if not, you've at least knocked out a chunk. Get in, get out, and decide if you want to keep going.

Example: Got lesson planning to do? Set a fifteen-minute timer. Focus on one subject or task, and when the timer goes off, take a five-minute break. You'd be surprised how much more you can get done in short bursts instead of trying to power through everything in a two-hour marathon.

Strategy 3: Make the Mundane a Game

Turn your most boring, repetitive tasks into a game. Compete with yourself, or better yet, reward yourself like the star you are. Can you clean up your desk in five minutes or less? Can you file papers before your favorite song finishes? ADHD brains thrive on fun, so gamify the stuff you usually dread.

Example: Your desk looks like a tornado hit it, and you're avoiding cleaning it up. Put on your favorite song and challenge yourself to beat the clock by cleaning it before the song ends. Boom—instant motivation and a cleaner workspace without the drag.

The Importance of Unplugging: Setting Clear Work-Home Boundaries

All right, this is where it gets real. As teachers, it's easy to blur the lines between work and home. You take home grading, respond to parent emails at 10 p.m., and find yourself Googling lesson ideas while watching Netflix. Let me be the first to say: STOP IT. Unplugging is the only way you're going to stay sane in this wild, time-consuming profession. The key is to draw a firm line between work and personal time. When you protect your energy and only give what you're paid for, you're setting a standard that values you. It works because, in doing so, you stay energized, focused, and fully present when it actually counts.

Strategy 1: Your End-of-Day Ritual

When the school bell rings, that's your cue that your workday is over. No more "just one more thing" or "I'll finish this real quick." Because we all know that one thing leads to another thing, and the next thing you know, the nightly custodian is there waxing the floors. Nope, no time to work overtime. It's time to shut it down.

When the school bell rings, your workday is over. Period. You need to have a ritual that signals to your brain, "Okay, we're done for the day." This could be something simple like cleaning up your desk, organizing tomorrow's lesson, or even just turning off your classroom lights with a *dramatic flourish*. My personal favorite is to set an alarm on my phone to Semisonic's "Closing Time." The point is, whatever ritual you choose, make sure it signals loud and clear: workday *over*.

Strategy 2: The 4 p.m. Rule

No work after 4 p.m. Period. End of story. I picked this time because most teachers' contracted hours end around then, but honestly? Feel free to make it even earlier. This is your hard-and-fast cutoff for all things school related. Grading? Nope. Lesson planning? Absolutely not. Those sneaky emails trying to guilt you into replying? Not today, Satan.

With all the fancy technology we have today, it's easy to turn off your school-related notifications at a certain time. That way, you won't be tempted by the dinging of your phone.

I know what you're thinking: "It's Friday. What do I do if I haven't gotten those lesson plans done by the end of day?" Calm down. All you have to do is just copy the plans from a previous week because your administrator will never know the difference. Kidding, but if you're feeling experimental, try it and let me know what happens.

On a serious note, if you still have time-sensitive items on your checklist at the end of the day, chances are you need to perfect your prioritization habits. If you need a refresher, refer back to the Matrix Breakdown section for guidance.

You deserve evening hours to do you—whether that means hitting the gym, binge-watching the latest Netflix drama, or just chilling with a glass of wine and absolutely no thoughts of next week's lesson plans. However, the average school system has *conditioned* us to believe that after-hours work is just part of the gig. But news flash—it doesn't have to be. Your time is yours. You'll be surprised how *freeing* it feels to set a workday boundary and stick to it.

Strategy 3: The Off Days

Weekends and holidays are sacred, honey. And you need to guard them like the password to your cell phone. Remember the beauty of having two whole days of freedom—forty-eight hours to do whatever the heck you want. And let's not forget holidays. Days off are your golden ticket, your vacation, your chance to remember that you're more than an educator. You're a real live human with hobbies, interests, and a life outside the school walls.

Use free time to catch up on sleep, spend time with family, and indulge in all the stuff you can't get to during the week. Turn your weekend into a self-care marathon. Eat a bougie breakfast and spend an hour with your favorite book or podcast. Maybe go out for a Saturday brunch with your crew, letting the mimosas flow as freely as the complaints about how hard it is to find a good substitute teacher. Take a spontaneous trip with the family—hit the beach, explore a new hiking trail, or visit that museum you've been eyeing. Or maybe just binge-watch that show you've been neglecting since September.

Whatever you do, don't check your email, and don't you dare go to that school. Everything will still be there on Monday, and you can handle it all when you're back in teacher mode.

Establishing a Daily Routine That Puts You First

Self-care isn't just a matter of enjoying our days off, though. And when I say self-care, I'm not just talking about fancy facials and massages (although they're amazing). I'm talking about creating a daily routine that prioritizes your mental health, your physical well-being, and your peace of mind.

One of those daily practices should involve activating the power of mindfulness. Before you roll your eyes, hear me out. Mindfulness isn't about sitting in a Zen garden for hours (unless you're into that, and if so, more power to you). It's just about taking a few moments each day to breathe, reset, and focus on the present. Try starting your day with five minutes of meditation, or even just a few deep breaths before you walk into your classroom. Trust me, the pause for self-care will make a difference.

In addition to mindfulness, try incorporating some form of exercise. I get it—squeezing in exercise is about as appealing as grading essays on a Sunday afternoon. But trust me, moving your body doesn't have to be a grand production. We're not aiming for fitness-model status here. A quick twenty-minute walk around the block, a YouTube yoga video, or even some dancing in your living room to your favorite playlist will do the trick.

If you're having trouble getting started with an exercise routine, think of it as nothing more complicated than time when you don't have to think about work. Exercise not only gives you energy, but it also clears your head, which means you'll show up to your classroom as a whole vibe, not a frazzled mess. And if you really get into it, you can be beach-body ready by the summer.

Now if you're an educator with a family, I know what you're thinking: "Me-time? Honey, where?" Between the kids, your partner, and the dog, you can't even sneak away for a potty break without someone calling your name. I get it. You're stretched thin at school, and then you come home to another round of responsibilities. Baby, you're juggling school and home, so you need me-time even more.

Pro tip: Take a warm bubble bath. That's right, a full-on spa moment in your own bathroom. Light some candles, add a little aromatherapy, and play some calming music. Or, if you're like me, set up your laptop and watch *Bridgerton* while you soak. Isolation and relaxation? Yes, please.

And if you're sitting there thinking, "There's no way this will work in my house," that's where boundaries come in. Remember the boundaries chapter? Apply it here too. Give yourself thirty minutes of freedom—whether that's after dinner, during your partner's shift with the kids, or when you lock the bathroom door with no shame. You need that time to recharge so you can show up fully for your family and your students.

Self-care isn't a luxury. It's nonnegotiable. You wouldn't let your phone battery run down to 1 percent every day and expect it to perform like it's brand new. So why do you think you can go nonstop without recharging yourself?

Rest and Recovery

No matter how well you structure your time, or how much self-care you incorporate into your daily life, you still need time to recover. That's right, ladies and gentlemen—you need sleep. I know some of y'all are out here running on five hours of sleep like it's normal, but can we stop pretending that's sustainable? Sleep is not a suggestion, it's a requirement. If you're running on empty, you can't expect to pour into your students, your family, or yourself. You wouldn't keep driving a car on *E* and wonder why it's breaking down, and it's the same thing with your body.

Rest is an act of resistance. In her book, *Rest is Resistance* (a personal favorite that changed my life), Tricia Hersey breaks it all the way down. Rest is not just about catching up on sleep. It's about reclaiming our time, our peace, and refusing to be part of a grind culture that tells us we have to hustle 24-7 to be worthy. You deserve rest, not just because you work hard, but because you're human.

And it's not just Tricia Hersey telling us that rest matters; many faith traditions value it as well. From the Judeo-Christian concept of the Sabbath to the Muslim day of Jumu'ah, to the mindful meditations of Buddhism, taking time to rest and restore your spirit is woven into spiritual practices across the world. Your body and soul need downtime to function at their best. If the universe is telling you to rest, why are you fighting it?

Make sleep a priority. Aim for a solid seven to eight hours a night. No more dragging through the day like a zombie, fueled only by caffeine and sheer willpower. Instead, set a bedtime and stick to it. Yes, a bedtime. You know, the time you wish your students abided by so they wouldn't come in dragging every morning? Or the one that your own children should have so that bubble bath would be easier to take without interruption?

Here's a sample evening to get your life in order after school (whether you're solo or juggling a family):

5:00 p.m. - Power Down from School Mode: If you're solo, take thirty minutes to clear your head. Whether it's a quick walk, some light stretching, or just listening to a podcast that has nothing to do with education, this is your time to shake off the day. If you have a partner and/or kids, communicate that you need thirty minutes of me-time when you first get home. Lock the bathroom door if you have to!

5:30 p.m. - Family Time / Personal Time: Spend this time catching up with your partner and/or kids, but keep it light. Don't bring the stress of the day into your home. If you're single, use this time to focus on something you enjoy—whether that's calling a friend, working on a hobby, or chilling with a good book.

6:30 p.m. - Dinner & Decompress: Enjoy a meal that nourishes your body and mind. You can cook together as a family or whip up something quick. And please, have your children help with cleaning up after dinner. If they can play with Legos and download apps on their tablets, they can load and start the dishwasher. Solo? This is a great time to throw on your favorite show while you eat. And as long as it is in your budget, there is no shame in food delivery.

7:30 p.m. - Wind-Down Routine: Now's the time to start slowing it all down. If you have kids, get them ready for bed and do a quiet activity like reading together. With a partner? Try playing a game like Scrabble or UNO. I hear bedroom games are pretty fun as well. Solo? Try doing something like a word search or listening to music. This is also a good time to do a quick brain dump—write down anything you need to remember for tomorrow so your mind isn't racing all night.

9:30 p.m. - Screens Off, Mind Off: At this point turn all screens off. I know it's tempting to scroll through Instagram one more time, but trust me, it's a trap. If you can, try meditation, deep breathing, or listening to an audiobook that helps you unwind.

10:00 p.m. - Lights Out: Yes, you—in bed, by 10 p.m. Don't argue with me! Whether you're with a partner, kids, or by yourself, this is the time to get those seven to eight hours in. Remember, your classroom will be there tomorrow, but you need to be at your best to show up for it.

When you make rest and sleep a priority, you're not just investing in yourself—you're investing in your students, your family, and everyone else who depends on you. So set those boundaries, establish your evening routine, and protect your rest.

The Takeaways

Reclaiming your time is about reclaiming your life. It's time to flip the script and prioritize you. Why? Because you can't give your best to anyone if your cup is empty.

By building time-management systems that actually work for your life and creating routines that serve *you*, you're setting yourself up for balance and success. Protect your time, protect your peace, and watch your world transform. Here are a few tips to take with you:

Identify and Eliminate Time-Wasters

- Stop saying "yes" to everything and overthinking every detail. Focus on what actually matters.

Master Time Management

- Prioritize your to-do list. Be sure to handle the important and urgent tasks first before losing valuable time on activities that can wait.

Unplug to Recharge

- Set a boundary for when work ends and personal time begins. No more grading papers in bed or answering emails at dinner. Recharge by resting and participating in extracurricular activities that matter to you.

Establish a Routine

- Create daily habits that allow moments for yourself. Whether it's journaling, exercising, or simply enjoying a cup of coffee without multitasking, the routine will create a good habit. You deserve a life that's balanced, joyful, and untethered from the classroom. At the end of the day, you're more than just a teacher. You're a whole person with dreams, goals, and a life worth living. Honor that.

Chapter 5

SIMPLIFYING YOUR WORKLOAD

See, What Had Happened Was: I Was Doing Way Too Much

Okay, so my third graders were about to start a unit on Japan, and I was hyped. If you know anything about me, you know I love me some culture. And I knew these kids hadn't seen much outside of their little rural Georgia bubble. So I had a brilliant idea to take them on a trip to Japan.

Now I didn't have "We're going to Tokyo" money. What teacher does? But I wasn't going to let that stop me. Oh no. I basically turned my classroom into "Japan in a box." I'm talking paper lanterns, art prints, DIY origami stations, and full-on calligraphy workshops. I even made a run to World Market to grab all the Japanese snacks I could afford. Yes, I was *that* teacher.

The kids were so into the experience, I'm pretty sure they thought I had a side gig as a tour guide. Meanwhile I was low-key dying. After weeks of staying late, working weekends, and spending nearly three hundred dollars of my own money, I was hanging on by a thread. Not to mention, my own family suffered. I pretty much ghosted them during this whole Japan saga.

The grand finale of the unit on Japan was an over-the-top cultural extravaganza. I had planned it all—games, music, everything. The cherry on top: I invited Japanese exchange students from a local university. I couldn't wait for my students to experience real cultural dialogue.

Everything about the culmination of the unit was simply amazing. The students were thrilled, and I loved seeing the joy on their faces. Even kids from other classes peeked in to see what was going on. But despite all of the magical experiences, the week still ended with me feeling exhausted and lying in bed all weekend.

Was it worth it? Eh. On one hand, pouring time and money into transforming my room for the Japanese unit created a magical, immersive experience. It was a true core memory for my students. They were excited, engaged, and genuinely curious, and this felt amazing. It made the content come alive in a way that worksheets and slides just couldn't. But the flip side? It drained my energy, stretched my budget, and left me wondering if all that effort was sustainable—or even expected—every time I wanted to spark interest.

The better question is this: Was there another way to get similar results with less headache? And to that, I enthusiastically say, "Yes!"

I know making a real impact in the classroom sounds easier said than done. You're probably side-eyeing me right now, thinking, "What you talking 'bout, Willis?" But I promise there is a way to make your workload feel a little less like a mountain and more like a molehill.

Streamline Lesson Planning Without Sacrificing Quality

If you're like the old me, you are probably spending more time *planning* lessons than actually teaching them. Seriously, I was out here like I was about to win an Academy Award for Best Lesson Plan. Every day was like crafting a masterpiece, complete with color-coded notes, handouts, and a Google Slides presentation that would make Pixar jealous. My lesson plans were a whole production.

But let me tell you something I learned after a few years of staying up till midnight planning lessons: No one's handing out Oscars for that. In fact, most of the time, your students don't even notice all the extra frills you might add to a lesson plan; they just want to understand the material without falling asleep. So let's talk about how to streamline your lesson-planning process, keep the quality high, and save you from spending your Sunday evenings in lesson-plan purgatory.

Strategy 1: Reuse and Recycle

First of all, there is *zero* shame in reusing lesson plans. None. If you've taught a topic before and it worked well, dust that bad boy off and use it again! I used to feel guilty, like reusing lessons was some kind of cheating. But why reinvent the wheel every single year? Recycle that lesson plan like it's one of the dozen Amazon boxes that were delivered to your house this week. If it's good, it's good.

The key to knowing which lesson plans are keepers is to keep things organized. Google Drive is your best friend. Create folders for every unit or topic you teach and save *everything* there. The key here is naming your folders by topics or units that make sense to *you*—so that even on your most tired or stressed-out day, you can quickly find that gem of a lesson plan. Trust me, "Unit 4: Fractions" or "Short Stories" is going to be easier to find than "Random PDF From Last Year."

Once you know a lesson plan worked well, make it part of your "greatest hits" collection. Keep a digital file of your tried-and-true lessons. The following year, when you're staring down a new unit and feeling overwhelmed, just pull up a lesson that you know worked, tweak it a little if necessary, and bam—you're ready to go. Instant stress relief. Less time panicking, more time chillin'.

Pro Tip: Hyperlink Your Resources

Here's a hack that'll make your future self want to give you a standing ovation: hyperlink everything in your lesson plans. If you have a video, worksheet, or any other resource that goes with the lesson, link it directly to your plan. This way, when you go back to it next year, it's all there. No searching through random files or scrolling through endless bookmarks. One click, and boom, you're ready to roll. It's like having your own digital assistant handing you everything you need in one neat package.

Pro Tip: Free Is Your Friend

Before you start buying resources, listen: Unless your administrator has given you some extra funds (and let's be real, that's a rare blessing), don't go spending your own money on every cute worksheet or bundle you see. That five dollars here, ten dollars there will add up *fast*, and before you know it, you'll have spent hundreds of dollars by the end of the school year. Instead, hit up Teachers Pay Teachers and Google for free resources. There are plenty of freebies out there if you just search for them. Remember, the keyword here is "free." You can find amazing stuff to enhance your lessons without breaking the bank.

Strategy 2: Batch Your Planning

Here's a trick I wish I'd learned when I was running around like a headless chicken as the director of curriculum at my district's board of education—batch your tasks. So rather than wearing yourself out with constant task switching—like reviewing a teacher's unit plan, then answering a district email, jumping into a meeting agenda, answering phone calls, and circling back to a budget spreadsheet, group similar work together. When batching in this way, you might dedicate an hour just to reviewing curriculum maps or block out your morning to finalize professional-development plans. When you stay in one mental lane, you work more efficiently, make fewer mistakes, and leave the day feeling way less scattered.

Trust me, when you've got a fast-paced environment, hard deadlines, and the superintendent breathing down your neck, you can't afford to be flying by the seat of your pants. I was juggling a million things—meetings, reports, presentations—and every day felt like a race to finish before something else landed on my plate. It wasn't sustainable. That's when I started batching, and it saved me from going completely under.

How to Make It Work:

- Set a Timer and Focus: Back when I was in graduate school, I would set strict time blocks. Whether this meant setting aside a two-hour chunk in the morning to write essays or an afternoon slot to review data, I dedicated that time to one task and only one. No multitasking, no switching between projects. I learned real quick that nothing gets done when you're pulled in ten directions at once. Same thing applies in teaching—give yourself a set amount of time, like Sunday afternoon or your planning period, and get laser-focused on planning the week's lessons. Just focus on that one task.
- Pre-Plan Resources: When I worked on curriculum, I made sure all my materials—whether for presentations, teacher training, or district initiatives—were ready to go before I even started putting things together. This is a must for teaching

too. Gather your worksheets, videos, readings, and online resources ahead of time and drop them in your lesson plan.

- Batch Work: Instead of planning day by day, start knocking out a week's worth of lessons at a time. Or better yet, plan for an entire unit if you can. When I had reports due for multiple schools or board meetings, I learned to focus on one school or project at a time rather than switching gears every day. This saved me from drowning in the chaos of constant last-minute scrambling. For teachers, it's the same principle—get into a rhythm by planning multiple lessons in one sitting, so you're not always playing catch-up.
- Take Breaks: I learned the hard way that you need to give yourself some breathing room. When I'm in the thick of deadlines, I make a point to step outside for a few minutes to clear my head. When you're batching your lessons, take little breaks. Do a quick breathing exercise, walk around the block, or even take a moment to just sit in silence. I keep music going in my office—something calm like classical or lo-fi beats when I need to focus. If I have a pile of tasks to knock out, I switch to something fast-paced like rap or pop to stay energized. The right playlist works wonders for keeping your head in the game.

Whether you're juggling district-wide initiatives or your classroom lesson plans, batching is the key to staying sane. Instead of dealing with the stress of piecing together tomorrow's lesson after a long day, knock out the entire week at once. It'll feel like a weight lifted off your shoulders, and you'll have more mental energy to actually enjoy teaching rather than just survive it.

Strategy 3: Use a Formula (But Make It Fun)

Listen, I love being creative as much as the next person, but there's no need to reinvent the entire structure of your lessons every single day. For me, my go-to lesson structure is like my secret sauce—it keeps things organized and effective and still leaves room for creativity. And the beauty of it? This formula works, and it's flexible enough for me to plug in different content, activities, or materials without having to reinvent the wheel each time. Having a go-to structure doesn't make your lessons boring. If anything, it helps you keep the creativity alive because you're not wasting time figuring out logistics. You can spend that energy thinking of fun content or engaging activities instead.

Here are the features common to every lesson plan I design:

1. When my students walk into the classroom, I always have a prompt ready on the board. It could be a quick five-minute solo writing prompt, a discussion question they tackle with a partner, or a brainteaser to get their minds working. This warm-up sets the tone and gets them settled without me having to wrangle them in.
2. Then we get to the heart of the lesson. This is where I jump in with direct teaching—whether it's a mini-lesson, some Q&A time, or even a bit of storytelling to get the message across. After that I focus on making sure students understand what's going on, so I give them either group work or solo time, depending on the day and the topic. And of course, music plays a role here too. I like to use something chill, like classical or coffee shop music during the intro and individual work time to keep the vibe calm and focused.
3. Finally we wrap it all up with a quick recap or reflection—something to reinforce what we've learned and tie it all together.

The structure is simple: intro prompt, direct teaching, check for understanding, and then a wrap-up. So find your formula. Whether it's something like mine or a different mix, sticking to a structure helps you plan smarter and faster. Trust me, your students will still get all the engagement and variety they need, but you won't be staying up late, stressed, trying to plan from scratch every day.

Strategy 4: Delegate, Delegate, Delegate

While I am in love with the outcome of an organized life—how it makes me feel and how I effectively function in it—I'd be lying to you if I said I enjoyed setting it all up. There is nothing I loathe more than tedious and boring tasks like organizing and cleaning up. It's just not in my DNA. So what do I do to avoid this torture? I get someone else to do it.

Despite popular belief, you do not have to do everything yourself. I know, shocking, right? But for some reason, we teachers have been conditioned to think we're supposed to be superheroes who do it all—teach, plan, grade, manage the classroom, decorate, and keep up with every extracurricular. News flash: There's no cape hiding under your cardigan. So it's time to start delegating.

Get Your Students Involved

Let's start with the obvious: Your students can help you out. Now I'm not saying they should be running the classroom (although, depending on the age and the day, maybe they could …). But there are definitely things they can handle that will take the load off of you. Assign classroom jobs—things like passing out papers, organizing materials, or even updating the calendar. Sharing work teaches students responsibility and saves you time.

If you're grading something straightforward—like a short quiz with clear right-or-wrong answers—let your students grade their own papers right there in class. This works especially well with secondary students, who often appreciate immediate feedback and the sense of autonomy it gives them. Not only does it save you from lugging a stack of papers home, but it also turns grading into a learning moment. Students can see exactly where they went wrong, ask clarifying questions on the spot, and start to take more ownership of their progress. It's efficient *and* educational.

And stop worrying about whether students will cheat! Set the expectation and use great behavior management. Have students trade their pencils for grading pens and let them grade away!

Share the Load with Colleagues

Look, there is no need for every single teacher to be out here creating separate lesson plans, activities, and projects for the same subject. If you've got a colleague who teaches the same grade or subject as you, collaborate! If your coworkers don't believe that sharing is caring, find a buddy online. Surely you know someone who knows someone who teaches the same subject.

Share lesson plans, swap materials, and even trade off on creating activities. It cuts your workload in half, and you still get fresh ideas from working with someone else.

Say "Yes" to Help

This one is big. When someone offers to help, *let them.* I used to be terrible at this because I thought I needed to prove I could do it all myself. But accepting help doesn't make you weak. It makes you smart. Whether it's asking for classroom support, leaning on a teaching assistant, or even having a friend give you a few ideas for a lesson, take the help when it's offered. You'll save yourself time and you'll avoid burnout.

Strategy 5: Let Go of Perfectionism

All right, we need to have a heart-to-heart about perfectionism. If you're anything like I used to be, you probably entered teaching with this idea that you had to be the perfect teacher—the one who had flawless lesson plans, beautifully decorated bulletin boards, and every student walking out of your classroom with a deep, life-changing understanding of the material.

But honey, perfectionism is a lie. And it's a lie that will run you into the ground if you let it. No one—*and I mean no one*—is a perfect teacher. We all have those days where the lesson doesn't go as planned, the students are off the rails, and we just want to curl up in a ball and hide. And that's okay.

1. **Embrace the "Good Enough" Approach.** One of the best things I ever did for my sanity was letting go of the need for everything to be perfect. Not every lesson needs to be a masterpiece. Not every classroom decoration needs to be Pinterest-worthy. Sometimes, *good enough* is exactly that—good enough. Focus on what's important (the learning) and let go of the rest. You'll feel a thousand pounds lighter, I promise.
2. **Give Yourself Permission to Make Mistakes.** Here's a secret: Your students don't expect you to be perfect. In fact, they probably appreciate it when you mess up because it shows them that it's okay to make mistakes. So stop holding yourself to impossible standards. You're human, and sometimes things are going to go wrong. The key is to learn from it, laugh it off, and keep moving forward.
3. **Stop Comparing Yourself to Other Teachers.** This is a big one. We've all been there—scrolling through Instagram, seeing those teachers with perfectly organized classrooms, elaborate lesson plans, and smiling students who seem like they're straight out of a catalog. And it's easy to feel like you're

falling short in comparison. Remember this: You don't know what's going on behind the scenes. Those teachers might be struggling with the same things you are. Plus, you bring your own unique strengths to the classroom that no one else can replicate. So stop comparing and start focusing on what *you* bring to the table. Trust me, it's enough.

Managing Full Production Lesson Plans

Not every lesson has to be Oscar-worthy. But even though I'm barefaced most days, every now and then I like to throw on a little eyeliner, shadow, and gloss for some extra pizzazz. Same goes for teaching. I'm all about adding a bit of magic here and there.

A classroom makeover or an elaborate lesson can be the educational equivalent of a bold red lip. It turns heads and makes everyone pay attention. These moments of effort can transform the mundane into something memorable. The learning sticks and kids walk out of the room feeling like rock stars. As a teacher you just have to remember you don't need to do everything yourself.

If you decide to give your class one of those "And the award goes to . . ." kind of lessons (cause remember that going all out is not mandatory), it does not need to be a one-teacher show. You think one person made *Wicked* happen? I think not. A full production requires a cast and crew. If you want to pull off an unforgettable lesson without feeling like you've aged ten years, you will need collaboration, resourcefulness, and a little advanced planning.

1. Two (or Three) Heads Are Better Than One

Why reinvent the wheel when your colleagues (or even parents) can help spin it with you? Team up with a fellow teacher—maybe the math teacher down the hall or the art teacher who loves a good project. Divide the workload: One of you plans, one sets up, and both teach.

Parents can also be your secret weapon. Send out a wish list email asking for props, supplies, or even time to help with setup or cleanup. People love a reason to feel useful (and let's be honest, they also love to peek inside your classroom).

2. Resources on a Budget

We're not out here trying to spend half our paycheck on a classroom transformation. Hit up Dollar Tree, thrift stores, or local Buy Nothing groups for inexpensive supplies. Libraries are gold mines for themed decorations, and many offer free educator kits. Also, don't sleep on DonorsChoose or writing a small grant—you'd be surprised how many people want to fund cool lessons for kids.

3. Plan Ahead

An Oscar-worthy lesson isn't something you throw together the night before. Start planning months in advance. Map out the materials you'll need, who's helping, and what tasks can be prepped early. Breaking it into chunks makes it manageable, and by the time your lesson day rolls around, you'll actually have the energy to teach instead of just collapsing in a chair.

4. Keep It Rare, Keep It Special

The magic only works when it's not overdone. Aim for one showstopping lesson per semester—just enough to keep things exciting without burning out. Students will look forward to it, and so will you.

Lesson Ideas to Spark Your Inner Spielberg

Math: Escape Room Challenge

Turn your classroom into an escape room where students solve math problems to unlock "doors" (boxes, envelopes, or QR codes). The story? They're astronauts trying to fix their spaceship before it crashes. Collaborate with the science teacher to add a STEM-related twist and ask parents to lend or donate items like black tablecloths (for space vibes) or LED lights. Free printables for puzzles and clues can be found online, and planning months ahead means you'll have time to test the game.

Math: Architecture Challenge

In this project students work in groups to design a sustainable, functional, and aesthetically appealing school building. Using mathematical concepts like area and perimeter and scale drawings from geometry and trigonometry, each group will create blueprints for the building. They must calculate material costs, floor space, and structural integrity. The final presentation involves both a physical model (created using materials like cardboard or 3-D printers) and a detailed cost analysis to present to a panel of local architects or city planners who will evaluate the practicality, efficiency, and innovation of the students' designs. This hands-on project connects math with real-world architectural design.

Math: Shark Tank Competition

Design a *Shark Tank: STEM Edition* project where student teams take on the role of start-up founders developing a product or service that solves a real-world problem—like optimizing traffic flow, designing eco-efficient buildings, or creating budget-friendly nutrition plans. Each team must use advanced math concepts—such as regression analysis, optimization, probability, and financial modeling—to build and justify their solution. They'll present their proposals to a panel of community stakeholders who act as the "sharks." This activity makes abstract math tangible and career-relevant, pushing students to apply their skills to real-life problems while developing persuasive communication, collaboration, and decision making.

Social Studies: Historical Time Machine

Transform your classroom into a time machine and take students back to a specific era—like ancient Egypt or the roaring twenties. Have stations where they can "experience" the time period: maybe through writing hieroglyphics or learning a jazz dance move. Collaborate with the art or drama teacher for set design and ask parents to donate or lend costume pieces. Start planning before the unit begins so you can integrate elements into your regular lessons leading up to the big day.

Civics: Branches of Government Simulation

Have students take on the roles of the legislative, executive, and judicial branches to explore how laws are made, enforced, and interpreted. Each group receives a current issue or fictional community problem—like regulating social media use in schools or creating a citywide recycling program. The legislative branch researches public opinion, debates ideas, and writes a bill. The executive branch decides whether to sign or veto the bill and explains how it would be implemented. The judicial branch evaluates whether the proposed law aligns with constitutional principles, civil rights, and legal precedent. Students experience firsthand how checks and balances work and how civic processes are rooted in negotiation, accountability, and public service.

Geography: Amazing Race Around the World

Pair your students up and have them complete geography challenges based on global destinations. Each group gets a passport and starts at a different "continent station" (complete with maps, flags, cultural items, and country clues). To advance to the next destination, they must solve puzzles like identifying countries based on matching landmarks to the correct region or using latitudinal and longitudinal coordinates to find mystery locations on a map. Add physical challenges like building a "Great Wall" out of blocks for an active twist. The first team to visit all the continents and correctly complete their travelogue wins a prize.

Language Arts: Literary Café

Turn your classroom into a cozy café where students "order" literary elements from a menu. Picture this: soft jazz playing, desks covered with tablecloths, and "servers" (you or a few parent volunteers) delivering tasks like analyzing themes, writing poetry, or creating character sketches. Bonus points for offering snacks (simple crackers or cookies work) to make the vibe authentic. Collaborate with the librarian for book-related decorations or borrow a coffee cart setup. Plan the literary café for a big review day or as a fun kickoff to a new unit and prep the "menu" items well in advance.

Language Arts: The Art of Advertisement

Assign your students a specific snack (e.g. soda, chips, candy) and have them design a persuasive advertising campaign to include a slogan, poster, jingle, and sixty-second commercial script. Provide a list of persuasive writing techniques for them to include, such as emotional appeal, bandwagon, testimonials, and loaded language. After they present to the class, have each student choose which advertisement was more convincing.

Literature: From Page to Performance

Have your students bring literature to life by selecting a key scene from a novel, such as *To Kill a Mockingbird*, and transforming it into a modern script. For example, students might choose the courtroom scene and creatively adapt it into a short film. Students can work in various roles, such as writers, directors, actors, and editors. This will deepen their literary analysis while fostering creativity, collaboration, and media literacy.

Science: Mad Scientist Lab

Transform your room into a science lab straight out of a movie: lab coats, goggles, bubbling beakers, and experiments galore. Students rotate through stations to test hypotheses—like making slime to learn the states of matter or using candy to model the solar system. Team up with another science or STEM teacher for extra hands and expertise. Ask parents for supply donations (food coloring, vinegar, etc.) and start gathering props early—Dollar Tree is your BFF here.

Science: Plant Detectives

Students can explore the fascinating world of botany through real-world observation and digital tools. They begin by venturing outside to investigate the plants around their school or neighborhood, using Google Lens to identify species and gather quick facts about each one. Back in the classroom, they analyze the data they collected, comparing leaf shapes, plant structures, and adaptations using science notebooks. Students then create a visual report or digital slide presentation that explains each plant's role in the ecosystem.

Science: Operation: Frog Edition

Students will step into the role of surgeons by combining the classic Operation game concept with a real frog dissection. Before the dissection students work in surgical teams to play a custom Operation: Frog Edition board game featuring a large felt frog mat with removable Velcro organs, plastic tweezers, and buzzers for wrong answers. Each team answers questions about frog anatomy, organ functions, and lab safety to "remove" or "replace" organs on the felt frog.

Surgical gloves, lab coats, and even face masks can be used as props to simulate a real surgical environment and build excitement. Once students transition to the actual dissection, they use dissection kits, labeled organ cards, and anatomy diagrams to guide their work.

In the end these lessons will stick with your students—and you—without sticking you with exhaustion. Work smarter, not harder, because the real magic happens when you're actually able to enjoy the teaching part.

The Takeaways

At the end of the day, simplifying your workload isn't about cutting corners or doing less, it's about being strategic with your time and energy so that you can show up as your best self for your students *and* yourself.

Simplify Lesson Planning Without Losing Impact

- Create templates, reuse and adapt past lessons, or collaborate with colleagues to share resources. Focus on quality over quantity—your lessons don't need to reinvent the wheel every time.

Organize Your Workspace

- A clutter-free workspace equals a clearer mind. Use organizers, label essentials, and keep what you need within arm's reach.

Teamwork Makes the Dream Work

- Delegate where you can. Let students help with organizing materials or cleaning up and lean on colleagues for group projects or coteaching ideas.

Embrace "Good Enough" over Perfect

- Perfectionism is exhausting and unnecessary. Give yourself permission to aim for "done well" rather than "flawless." Your students need a present, energized teacher, not a perfectionist running on empty.

Remember you don't have to do it all, and you definitely don't have to do it all perfectly. The goal is to work smarter, not harder, and to create space for yourself in the midst of the chaos. Because at the end of the day, you're more than just a teacher—you're a human being who deserves balance, peace, and a workload that doesn't leave you feeling overwhelmed.

So go ahead, simplify your life. You've got this.

Chapter 6

BUILDING A PRODUCTIVE, SUSTAINABLE ROUTINE

See, What Had Happened Was: My Life Was a Hot Mess

Let me take you back to a chapter in my life I call "Hot Mess Express," where every single day felt like a rat race. Many of you can probably relate to this life. You know, the alarm goes off like the starting gun at the Kentucky Derby. "And . . . we're off!" I'm up, stumbling, and immediately trying to figure out what day of the week it is while speed-walking to the shower. As the water runs over my body, I'm mentally running through my checklist of the day.

Step one: Wake my son up because, for some reason, the alarm can only get his attention if it's to watch the premier of some new anime.

Step two: Bang on the bathroom door and remind my son to actually *take* a shower instead of running the water while sitting on the toilet.

Step three: Start the Keurig and simultaneously scan the pantry for breakfast bars.

Step four: the lunch situation. We're talking about a high-stakes decision-making moment here because neither of us is willing to roll the dice on whatever cafeteria mystery meal awaits. And so there I am, yelling for my son to come downstairs so he can slap together a ham and cheese sandwich, throw some chips in a plastic bag, and find a juice box. And my lunch is basically whatever leftovers I can throw into a Tupperware container or else it's an overpriced lunch delivery.

Step five: odds and ends. As if I didn't have enough going on, my son remembers the field trip permission slip that needs my signature. Of course he doesn't have a pen handy. I place the uncharged laptop in my bag, holding the absolute terror that I might've misplaced my charger *again*. Meanwhile my kid's asking me questions like, "Mom, can Kolten spend the night?" and I'm thinking, "Boy, let's just try to make it to the car with your shoes on," which, by the way, has sadly not occurred on multiple occasions.

Step six: departure. By the time we're racing out the door, I'm basically hurdling over a pile of toys and my last ounce of patience. We screech into the school parking lot with a minute to spare—because life knows I'm going to clock in just late enough to make a point. I step into my classroom, slap on a smile, and tell myself I'm good. But who am I kidding? I'm still catching my breath as the bell rings and I'm motioning for the students to enter. And everyone is clueless to the Olympics-level dash that got me here.

After a morning like that, does the actual teaching day go fine? Yeah, kinda. Do the kids learn? Of course. But am I wiped out by lunchtime? Absolutely. Why? Because much like my morning, my school day has become a juggling act of teaching and managing other work responsibilities in the end. Everything flows in and out of each other, and it somehow managed to flow right into my home where I would start the madness again the next day.

It's like a wise person once said: "How you start is how you finish." And on days like the ones in that "Hot Mess Express" chapter of my life? I was barely finishing at all. But life doesn't have to feel like a never-ending sprint from alarm clock to classroom. You don't have to roll into your day out of breath, clutching coffee like it's an oxygen tank.

Imagine waking up with enough time to actually taste your breakfast, send your kid off with both shoes *and* a smile, and walk into work calm, collected, and ready to face whatever awaits. You greet your coworkers with genuine warmth, and you open your door to an already prepped classroom—agenda on the board, worksheets in neat stacks, and assignments already scheduled to post on Google Classroom. Your students walk in, and you have time to chat about their weekend before beginning the official lesson of the day. That's the life we're aiming for here.

This chapter is going to show you how to transform those rushed, chaotic mornings into moments that set you up for success. Throughout, I'll provide you with small routines and mindset shifts that ultimately make a big difference at work. Get ready, because the marathon mornings end here. Instead you'll wake up feeling refreshed and ready, no longer overwhelmed by a cluttered to-do list, and you will have time to check in with yourself before diving into the day. With small adjustments, your mornings will shift from frantic to focused. This new flow will allow you to step into work with a calm and confident energy that carries you through the day.

Strategy 1: Create a Rhythm for the Day

Any Coldplay fans in the house? Okay, think about their hit song "Viva La Vida." The strings rise and fall in perfect harmony, the drums keep a steady march in the background, and Chris Martin's smooth voice enters at just the right time singing, "I used to rule the world . . ." Every element of the song works in sync. But imagine if the strings played over the vocals, the drums sped up randomly, or Chris stumbled over the lyrics. It would be horrible, and the magic would be lost. That's how life feels when your day is out of rhythm: chaotic and scattered.

When each part of your day—work, rest, family, and you-time—has its own space and time, your life flows like a perfectly orchestrated song. When you find a routine, life as a teacher is not about rushing through everything or multitasking until you're burned out. Routine is about knowing when to focus, when to relax, and when to give yourself a moment to just breathe. The beauty is that your rhythm doesn't have to follow anyone else's tempo; it's yours to create. And when you find it, your day will feel as balanced and uplifting as your favorite song.

Right now you may be feeling a bit skeptical. You're probably saying to yourself, "But has she ever faced a class of twenty-five balls of energy or tried to squeeze a ten-minute lunch in between student meltdowns?" The answer is yes. I'm a witness that we aren't just managing our own lives, we are also tasked with managing the lives of tiny humans and hormonal teenagers, who sometimes believe every minor inconvenience is the end of the world, for eight hours each workday.

But what if I told you that building a productive and sustainable routine could actually save you from losing your mind? We're talking about creating a rhythm that feels productive, that balances the chaos of the day, and gives you space to breathe without always feeling like you're playing catch-up. Oh, honey, it's totally achievable. Let me be a witness and share a few of my secrets.

The Morning Mindset

The key to owning your day starts with owning your morning. Now no one's saying you have to wake up at 5 a.m., run five miles, and chug a green juice unless that's genuinely your thing. For the rest of us, a morning routine that feels doable and fits our lives can make all the difference in setting a tone that works.

Start with something that centers you, whatever that may be. For me it's stepping outside with a good drink in hand, feeling that fresh morning air. Some days it's coffee; other days it's ice water, but the routine itself grounds me. Your morning ritual could be five minutes of peace away from your family and electronics, a quick stretch, or even just making your bed to signal a fresh start.

Dancing to Your Own Beat

Teaching is a lot like a tango—it's all about finding the right steps and moving in sync with the flow of the day. You don't have to rush through every move, and sometimes, a little pause can be just as powerful as a dramatic spin. Start by noticing when your energy (and the students' energy) peaks and when it dips. Just like a dance, you need to know when to lead with enthusiasm and when to take a moment to catch your breath. The key is to keep the flow, not by packing every minute but by letting your rhythm guide you through moments of connection, teaching, and even a little improvisation. Once you find your groove, you'll glide through your day like you're on the dance floor, staying energized without missing a step.

The end of your day is just as crucial as the start, so take time to intentionally close out each teaching day. Think of it as your grand finale—a final spin or a confident bow that signals the end of the performance. Don't rush out the door. Instead, make it a graceful exit, reflecting on what went well and setting yourself up for the next day. By creating this rhythm at the end of your day, you're leaving the floor with poise. This helps you step away from work with a sense of accomplishment and mentally prepares you to fully embrace your personal time, ensuring that work doesn't follow you home. It's a small but effective habit that protects your energy and promotes work-life balance.

By setting a rhythm while teaching and structuring your end-of-day routine, you create boundaries that protect your time and energy. These intentional habits help you maintain focus, stay energized throughout the day, and ensure that your evenings are restful and rejuvenating. Over time these small but consistent shifts will lead to a sustainable routine that not only makes teaching more manageable but enriches your overall well-being

Small Wins That Involve the Family

- **With Young Kids**: Include them in your morning routine in a simple, calming way. You might sit together for a few minutes on the couch for "quiet time" with a cozy blanket, a book, or some simple meditation music. You're taking your moment while they get used to a calm start too.
- **With School-Age Kids**: Let them be part of your routine by making the morning feel like a "team huddle." You can start with a family breakfast (This can literally be cereal and milk). For your grounding moment, have everyone share one thing they're excited about for the day (You might find out about that field trip permission slip an hour earlier). This provides a light way to connect while reinforcing a positive mindset.
- **With Older Kids or a Busy Spouse**: With older kids or a spouse, it is likely that everyone has their own unique way of starting their morning. However, you could set up a quick family routine that lets everyone contribute without much fuss. For example, everyone can gather in the kitchen for a few minutes before heading out. That way you get a dose of connection but still have a personal morning moment to recharge yourself.

Strategy 2: Work Smarter, Not Harder

Now, once you've taken your moment to consider the broad rhythms of a routine, it's time to get down to business. You need a plan for the workday that works for you—one that doesn't make you feel like you're on a hamster wheel going nowhere.

Back in the 90s, I remember spending weeks playing *Super Mario Brothers*, trying my hardest to beat King Koopa. I got tips from friends and memorized patterns. I tried everything, but I was barely making any progress.

Then my little brother came along. And in just a few hours, he was already breezing through the levels with extra lives and defeating Koopa like it was nothing. My jaw was on the floor! What I later learned was that he had access to a cheat code. He got the same results, but without all the pain and frustration.

We've all heard the phrase "work smarter, not harder." It's the key to surviving this chaotic world we're all trying to juggle. Like my brother's cheat code, a good routine is *also* about finding the hacks that let you cut through the mess and get to the good stuff faster. So instead of busting your brain trying to do everything the hard way, find an easier path.

I know, I know. There's something weirdly satisfying about working yourself to the bone. You feel accomplished, like you've proved you're doing something in life. But honey, working hard doesn't make you more productive. It just makes you tired.

Working smarter is about being intentional with your time and energy, cutting out the fluff, and focusing on what actually matters. So maybe it's time to take that shortcut and stop feeling guilty about it.

Planning

One of the biggest tools that can help you work smarter is planning. I know what you're thinking: "Girl, my whole life is planning." And my reply to that is, "Honey, not all planning is created equal." If your planning sessions leave you feeling like you just ran a mental marathon and still can't find the finish line, it's time to flip the script.

First off, I'm going to let you in on the little secret of batch planning. Just like with batched lesson planning, as we discussed last chapter, try sitting down once a month and planning out the big picture. Yes, the *whole* month.

Get yourself a planner that works for you—digital, paper, sticky notes on your wall, whatever gets your organizational juices flowing. Dedicate an hour once a month to outlining your major goals and lessons. You don't have to nail down every tiny detail but get the framework solid.

Now that's not to say you won't need to tweak things as you go (because let's be real, something always goes left), but at least you're not starting from scratch every week. You're setting yourself up to walk into each week feeling like you've already got it handled.

Bonus Tip: Some people are all about bullet journals, while others are devoted to Google Calendar. Me? I keep it simple. I use a physical planner with one black pen and a highlighter for emphasis—no need for a rainbow of colors here.

For major stuff, especially anything with a deadline or involving other people, I set an alert on Google Calendar to stay on track. The key is to make your planning easy and realistic. If it feels like a chore, you won't stick to it.

Time Blocking

Okay, so a few years ago, I met this friend in a women's leadership program—a true powerhouse. She had the aura of a goddess mixed with a presidential presence. College professor, entrepreneur, national speaker, grant writer—this woman was unstoppable, and every time she achieved something, she was onto the next thing. And with all of this, she was married with two children.

One day I texted her about catching up, and she excitedly offered a day and time. I confirmed. Noon rolled around on the specific day, and right on the dot, she called. I was shocked and teased her about the preciseness, and she explained that our call was placed on her calendar with a notification.

We had a great chat, but she kept it direct and, after twenty-nine minutes exactly, wrapped it up. I teased her again about her extreme structure, and she explained that she schedules her whole life to avoid wasting time.

At first, I was like, "Wait, did my friend just treat me like a business meeting? Should I be offended?" But the more I thought about it, the more I saw the wisdom in her strategy. Now while I don't think I'll ever plan my life down to the minute, there's something to be said for the power of time blocking.

Time blocking is like putting your day into neat little Tupperware containers—everything gets its space, and nothing spills over. Start by looking at your daily tasks and grouping them into blocks of time: lesson planning, grading, parent communication, and yes, even you-time.

Need to grade papers? Block out forty-five minutes after school and then walk away when the timer goes off. Planning lessons? Carve out an hour during your prep period or early in the week so you're not scrambling to finish on Thursday night. The key is to stick to the blocks—no multitasking or sneaky emails during your lunch break!

By compartmentalizing your day, you'll not only get more done but also free up energy to enjoy life outside of work. There's a time for work and a time for play, and they don't have to overlap.

Strategy 3: Set Realistic Expectations

We all want to be the teacher who's *on top of everything.* Some days you're going to crush it, and other days you're going to be just getting by, and that's *okay.* Stop trying to be superhuman. Give yourself some grace and set goals that reflect *your reality.*

Look at everything you've got going on this week. If your afternoons are packed with doctor's appointments and soccer practices, acknowledge that, by the evening, your energy levels will be low. Set manageable tasks; save the big projects for a slower week.

And remember it's not just your schedule—if your kids are dealing with tests, sports tournaments, or big family events, you might need extra energy to support them. Balance isn't about doing everything; it's about knowing when to dial back. Perfection is a myth. You're here to make a difference, not to run yourself ragged.

Reminder: Just Say "No"

I'm sure you remember Chapter 2, on responding with a guilt-free "no." If you have begun practicing this art, know I'm smiling real big and high-fiving you in spirit. But if you're still waiting for that first "no" or are haunted by guilt when you say it, then we've got some work to do.

Saying "no" isn't just a way to set your priorities, it's a way to manage other people's expectations of you. If you can't say "no," balance flies out the window. Don't overcommit to extra duties, committees, or meetings that drain your time. Remember your time is precious, and you are allowed to protect it. If someone asks you to take on more than you can handle, hit them with a polite but firm response. And walk away guilt-free.

Keeping Your Personal Life Sacred

I'm sure you feel like work sometimes takes over your life. Maybe you've left the classroom but still find yourself answering emails on a Friday evening or tweaking lesson plans on a Sunday night.

I've been there, but I finally found my groove with boundaries, balance, and giving myself the freedom to shut down. This is why I'm going to give you a sneak peek into my life. What you're about to read is *real life.* A hundred percent legit. If you need receipts, you can probably find the highlights on my social media page.

Friday, October 25

2:15 p.m.: Planning period hits, and I'm locked and loaded. I create my to-do list and set my time for one hour, no overtime allowed. First move? Borrow a coworker's lesson plan template. Why reinvent the wheel when you can cosign a good one?

I remix the plans and add hyperlinks to any games or worksheets I plan to include. Next I schedule assignments on Google Classroom, send worksheets to the copier, and organize my worksheets into folders I've labeled by day of the week.

When the timer dings, there are two stacks of ungraded papers staring at me. Did I consider grading them? Yes. Did I actually grade them? Not today, Satan. That timer is my boundary notification. No "just one more thing" spirals that turn into sunset exits for me.

3:15 p.m.: The planning period is officially over, and it's time for tutorial hour. Students have the option to come for twenty-five minutes of extra help, and most of them are either busy with after-school activities or socializing in the courtyard. But of course one lone student strolls in with ten minutes left, like she's casually deciding whether she wants help or just to say "hello." Bless her heart, because she's getting a crash course in speed tutoring. I take her last question at the two-minute mark. And then, *ding, ding, ding*—my pack-up alarm goes off at exactly 3:40. It's like the reminder that *my* time is precious too. So with the grace of a teacher who knows boundaries, I bid her farewell.

3:40 p.m.: I'm out the door like a ninja, making a beeline for the parking lot. I've got a twenty-minute drive home, and I use that time wisely—phone calls to my family and friends and listening to a book from my audio library.

4:00 p.m.: By the time I pull up at home, unpack my car, and change into my comfy clothes—yoga pants and a T-shirt—there's still some sunlight left. I love a good walk after a day in the classroom. After that mental breather, I'm faced with the critical decision: leftovers from last night? Cook what I took out of the freezer (that'll probably never happen)? Or should I just give in and order delivery? And while I ponder my culinary fate, I add to my growing grocery list. It's one less thing to worry about while I'm figuring out whether I'm eating lasagna or ordering Chinese.

6:00 p.m.: With the day's teaching done, I have fully transitioned to the next phase of my life. I'm a teacher by day, and I shine by night. After a long, hot bubble bath with my aromatherapy candles, I wrap myself in my comfiest robe. I pour a glass of Moscato and scroll social media like the relaxed goddess I am.

Dinner? General Tso's chicken delivered to my throne (aka the couch). Entertainment? A Rachel Cho comedy special with a friend because nothing caps off a Friday like laughing until your stomach hurts. By 10 p.m. it's lights out for me. I'm fully satisfied and ready for dreamland.

Saturday, October 26

8:00ish a.m.: No alarm. I wake up when my body says so. I'm talking natural, peaceful, just-right timing. Cue a little journaling and a casual morning scroll on my phone that turns into unnecessary online shopping. Don't judge me.

9:30 a.m.: Still in pajamas I wander to the kitchen and make a slow, lazy breakfast: avocado toast with everything bagel seasoning and a cup of coffee.

10:00 a.m.: I finally move to the couch. The plan was to do "one load" of laundry. Instead I alternate folding towels with deep dives into social media reels and "just one episode" of *Pop the Balloon,* a dating show where basic characteristics are somehow red flags.

1:00 p.m.: I take a nap. Why? Because I learned I don't need to justify my naps.

3:30 p.m.: I finally rally. I switch the laundry again (yes, that same load), tidy the living room a bit, and light a candle to make it *feel* like I did something.

5:00 p.m.: Time to transform. I cue up a getting-ready playlist and start doing my makeup in between dance breaks and solo karaoke. Tonight I'm going out for a Halloween party. I'm Wendy—from the burger joint. Red wig, freckles, that iconic blue dress with an apron. I look cute too!

7:45 p.m.: I arrive at the costume party and immediately spot Han Solo flirting with a sassy Princess Leia, a sexy Barbie and Ken couple, and Cleopatra complete with a man feeding her grapes. I feel proud to be among adults who clearly want to have as much fun as kids.

8:00–10:30 p.m.: I eat a mixture of fancy and creepy hors d'oeuvres, sip themed cocktails, and laugh until my sides hurt. There's a costume contest. I don't win, but it was fun to watch.

11:00 p.m.: Back home, face washed, wig off, and pajamas back on. It's way past my normal bedtime. I fall into bed feeling the good kind of tired—like I did nothing and everything all in one day.

Sunday, October 27

9:00 a.m.: I wake up, glance at the sunlight slipping through the blinds, and immediately realize I'm not twenty-two anymore. My body feels it. I roll over and decide to grant myself another hour (or two) of sleep.

11:15 a.m.: I finally crawl out of bed and wrap myself in a robe. No rush. No plans.

12:42 p.m.: A friend texts me out of the blue. She scored last-minute tickets to the Atlanta Symphony Orchestra for tonight. I don't even hesitate. Yes please. I need a little beauty in my life.

3:30 p.m.: We slide into our seats just as the lights dim. The music begins, and for a little while I feel completely at peace.

5:00 p.m.: I meet up with a girlfriend for a dinner that turns into a full-on girlfriend recharge session.

9:45 p.m.: I double-check that my alarm is set for 6:30 a.m. Reality is calling. But at least I answered the weekend with rest and music.

After years of overcommitting and running on empty, I've learned that giving myself space to prioritize my own needs is essential for maintaining balance. I aim for eight hours of sleep because I know when I'm well rested, I'm able to show up fully in every part of my life. I also try to eat healthily, but I'm not shy about treating myself now and then. A little indulgence—whether it's a favorite snack of gummy bears or a comfort meal—serves as a reminder that I deserve those small moments of joy. Exercise plays a part in this balance too, though I'm not exactly a gym fanatic. I'm more of a simple walk kinda girl. I enjoy those semiquiet moments before diving back into the chaos of life.

Sometimes I crave deep conversations and the recharge that comes from being with people who get me. Other times I need my solitude to reflect, recharge, or just escape into my own world. Having the freedom to ebb and flow between those two is crucial. Because predictability can sometimes become a little too much, I have learned to lean into spontaneity. Whether it's deciding to take an impromptu detour or simply switching things up to keep my days interesting, embracing a little unpredictability is what keeps me ready for whatever life brings next.

The Takeaways

It's important to establish a blueprint for building a productive, sustainable routine that *actually* works. And since we've discussed cheat codes, here's the cheat sheet for what we covered in this chapter:

Create Your Daily Rhythm

- Think of your day like a playlist, with every moment having its own vibe and purpose. Start strong, ride the flow, and make sure there's time to slow it down for yourself.

Work Smarter, Not Harder

- Stop overcomplicating your life! Use tools like planners, apps, and templates to save time and energy. You don't need to reinvent the wheel every day. Just make sure it's rolling in the right direction.

Find Your Work-Life Balance Groove

- Whether it's saying "no" to that extra committee, setting a strict *no work emails after 5 p.m.* rule, or just taking a real lunch break, you must have balance in your life.

Keep Work Outta Your Personal Life

- Remember to lean on those boundaries you set. That means leaving your papers at school, your laptop closed after-hours, and your brain on "me-time" once you're at home. Don't forget to plan a few outings and have fun doing you.

Remember that routine is not about being perfect or having it all together every day; it's about finding a rhythm that allows you to do your best work without losing yourself in the process.

Part 3

RECONNECTING WITH YOUR PASSION FOR TEACHING

Chapter 7

REMEMBERING YOUR "WHY"

See, What Had Happened Was: I Thought I Had It All Figured Out

At nineteen I was pretty sure I had life all figured out. I was a biology major, laser-focused on becoming an orthodontist. Orthodontists are known to make good money, so I thought I'd have a beautiful life of straightening smiles and collecting big checks.

I was also deeply involved in my church, practically living at my university's Baptist Student Union. So when my church members suggested a spring break mission trip to West Chicago, I was in. The plan? Restore a neighborhood, build a volunteer dentist office, paint some houses, and start an after-school club for latchkey kids. A week of hard work and payment in "blessings." I figured, why not?

What I didn't expect was that the highlight of the mission trip would be the kids. I had never worked with children in my life, but it felt so natural. Somehow spending my afternoons with a bunch of loud, curious, and chaotic children became the thing I looked forward to the most about the trip. These kids had so much energy, but they had a way of wearing you out and filling you up at the same time.

Then came the eye-opener. One day I rode the bus as it dropped the kids off in their neighborhood. This neighborhood gave a whole new meaning to "run-down." These kids were living in homes that needed more than a little TLC. And the sadder thing was knowing no parents would be home until hours later because of their late-shift jobs. These kids needed a serious intervention—something or someone to show them that their world could be bigger than what they'd seen so far.

I had my "aha" moment right there. I knew education could change the trajectory of their lives. My parents had drilled the importance of education into me since I could talk, and I had already seen the fruits of teaching. I wanted these kids (and all children) to know that same truth—that knowledge could open doors they didn't know existed. So I kissed my biology major goodbye, waved a dramatic farewell to orthodontics, and walked into education with open arms.

Fast-forward twenty-three years, and here I am. I've loved nearly every minute of my career in education (although sometimes I wonder about that orthodontist pay). I love seeing kids light up when they get it, helping them figure out who they are, and showing them how to be decent humans. Teaching feeds my soul in ways I didn't even know it needed feeding.

Why am I still teaching after all these years? Because people—especially the little ones—are my thing. Teaching is one of those gifts I can give the world. So here I am, spreading knowledge and good vibes, keeping it real, and still finding joy in every chaotic moment in this world of education.

But let's be honest: Teaching is not always rainbows and butterflies. There are days when you feel like you're shouting into the void and your students are more interested in their phones than your carefully crafted lessons. Trust me, I've been there—standing in front of a class with that sinking feeling, questioning my life choices. The struggle is real, and it's easy to lose sight of your "why" when you're caught in the grind.

A few years back, I hit one of those rough patches. I felt like I was going through the motions—showing up, doing my best, but not really connecting with my students. I'd left my passion at the door, and all that was left was a tired teacher fighting the daily battles of classroom management and curriculum compliance.

One particularly tough day, I left school feeling defeated. I collapsed on my couch, put my phone on "Do Not Disturb," and cried. I questioned whether I still had what it took to be an effective teacher.

That's when I stumbled upon my memory box. It's just an old shoebox filled with pictures of former classes, handwritten notes from students, and a few notes I had written myself. What I didn't realize as I was tossing the items in the box each year was that it would be filled with the fruits of my labor, dreams, and aspirations. I wanted to inspire my students and create a space where learning felt like an adventure, and those notes served as a wake-up call. It was time to reconnect with my "why" and reignite that passion.

The concept of "finding your 'why'" has become a bit of a buzz phrase, but at its core, it's one of the most powerful guiding principles in both life and work. Your "why" is not just about what you do, but why you do it. It's the reason you show up day after day, even when things get hard. For teachers especially, identifying that inner "why" is crucial because the work isn't always easy, glamorous, or immediately rewarding. But when you're anchored in a meaningful purpose, you feel more motivated, more fulfilled, and more resilient in the face of challenges.

I believe that every one of us is born with unique gifts and talents, and your "why" is often rooted in those gifts. Maybe you have the ability to inspire curiosity, to listen deeply, to create structure, to bring joy, or to make people feel safe. Those talents aren't meant to sit dormant; they're designed to be poured into others. For teachers this often looks like using your gifts not only to educate, but to elevate—to build confidence, unlock potential, and light a spark in your students. Your "why" isn't a job title or a task on your to-do list. It's the underlying mission that connects your skill set to someone else's growth. And in doing so, you grow too.

The important thing to remember is that everyone's "why" will look different. Some teachers are called to be encouragers, some are master explainers, some thrive on creativity, and others are driven by structure and strategy. There's no one-size-fits-all purpose, and that diversity is what makes a school community powerful. The key is learning how to identify what fuels you, then shaping your teaching practice around that. When you teach from a place of purpose, it becomes more than just a job—it becomes a calling. And when you're walking in your calling, even the hardest days can't take away your joy.

Rekindling the Flame

So how do you rekindle that flame when it feels like it's flickering? One strategy is deep reflection. Think back to that glorious moment when you decided to become a teacher. What was it that inspired you? Maybe it was your former teacher who lit up the classroom like a Broadway star. Perhaps it was that feeling of being the guiding light for students who needed a little extra love and encouragement.

Although the mission trip I took to Chicago was the turning point in my career, I actually believe my first-grade teacher, Mrs. Inman, planted the seeds for me becoming a teacher. Mrs. Inman was the embodiment of love and enthusiasm. She felt like a grandma and a sorceress all in one. I mean, she had this magical way of turning mundane lessons into interactive escapades that kept us engaged. And I still remember how she started each day at the grand piano that was in the corner of the room. "Good morning to you! Good morning to you! We're all in our places with sunshiny faces!" she'd sing.

It was in her classroom that I realized the power of teaching and the joy that comes from igniting curiosity in young minds. Mrs. Inman didn't just teach; she inspired. And somewhere along the way, I wanted to be just like her. And my proof can be found in a journal my mother made me complete at the end of each school year. In the journal, my seven-year-old self stated that I wanted to be a teacher.

But it wasn't just admiration—it was a deep sense that teaching was where my gifts and joy intersected. From an early age, I was a writer with a wild imagination, a lover of play, and a full-blown extrovert who came alive when connecting with others. I wasn't the kid who played house—I played school, complete with handmade worksheets, story time, and interactive games for an audience of baby dolls. When I was older, I gravitated toward jobs that allowed me to engage with people—whether it was working in customer service at grocery stores, waiting tables with a smile, or serving as a resident advisor planning weekend outings for overwhelmed college freshmen. Even as a Sunday school volunteer, I'd tell dramatic Bible stories like we were on Broadway. Teaching allowed me to blend my love for connection, creativity, performance, and learning all into one beautiful pursuit. Even now it's the place where I feel most fully myself.

Your "why" is your superpower. It's the driving force that will help you navigate the ups and downs of teaching. When the going gets tough, remember the passion that led you here. Reflect on the moments that ignited that fire in you and let them guide you through the challenging times.

As you embark on this journey of remembering your "why," keep that passion alive. You are not just a teacher; you are a beacon of hope, a source of inspiration, and a champion for your students. The world needs educators like you—passionate, dedicated, and ready to make a difference. So grab your coffee, put on your favorite playlist, and let's go remind ourselves why we fell in love with teaching in the first place!

Exercises for Reconnecting with Your Sense of Purpose in Teaching

All right, folks, now that we've unpacked the emotional suitcase of why we got into this whole teaching gig, let's get into the nitty-gritty of how to actually reconnect with that sense of purpose. Think of these exercises as your personal road map, leading you back to the joyful and vibrant educator you once were—or maybe still are deep down inside. So roll up your sleeves, and let's dive into some hands-on activities that will help you rediscover your teaching spark.

1. Starting Reflections

Every teacher's journey is different. Here are a few prompts to help you (and possibly your colleagues) remember why you entered this profession:

1. What inspired you to become a teacher? Write down the people, experiences, or moments that motivated you to choose this path.
2. Describe a moment in your teaching career that made you feel like a rock star. What happened, and how did it make you feel?
3. List three qualities you admire in the teachers who inspired you. How can you embody those qualities in your own teaching?
4. What are your goals for this school year? How do these goals align with your "why"?
5. Reflect on how you can make a positive impact on your students this year. What actions will you take to ensure your students feel valued and inspired?

2. The Passion Board

If you prefer to communicate in images rather than words, another powerful way to reconnect to your "why" is to create a passion board. A passion board is a visual display of everything that inspires you about teaching. Grab a corkboard, some magazines, and a good pair of scissors. Cut out images and phrases that resonate with your teaching philosophy and your goals in your classroom. Put the passion board somewhere you'll see it every day—a little reminder that you're not just a teacher; you're a changemaker. Each time you glance at it, you'll be reminded of why you started this journey in the first place.

Reflecting on your impact can be a game changer. It reminds you that teaching isn't just about the curriculum; it's about building relationships and nurturing growth. It's those little moments—the smiles, the thank-yous, and the lightbulb realizations—that make it all worth it.

3. The Gratitude Wall: A Visual Reminder of Impact

If you need a tangible reminder of your impact, it can't hurt to build your very own Gratitude Wall. Grab a poster board or an empty wall in your classroom (if you can get away with it) and start filling it with notes of appreciation from your students. You can encourage them to write thank-you notes or share their favorite lessons.

Now you might be thinking, "A Gratitude Wall? Really? There's simply no room for 'extras' like this when I have to post my curriculum standards and academic benchmarks." But hear me out! There's something profoundly uplifting about seeing the tangible impact you have on your students' lives. When you're knee-deep in grading or feeling the weight of the world on your shoulders, take a moment to look at your Gratitude Wall. Each note is a reminder of your influence and why you chose to become a teacher in the first place.

And let's be honest: Who doesn't love a little wall decor that reminds you of the good vibes? Plus, the Gratitude Wall is a great way to foster a positive classroom culture.

4. Revisit Your Vision Statement

Okay, let's get reflective. If you don't already have a personal vision statement, it's time to create one. This statement should encapsulate who you are as an educator and what you hope to achieve in your classroom. Think of it as your personal teaching manifesto.

Take a moment to jot down your core values—what principles guide your teaching? What do you believe is the purpose of education? Now use those thoughts to craft a vision statement.

For example, mine might read something like: "I strive to create a nurturing, inclusive environment where every student feels valued and inspired to explore their passions."

Once you've written your vision statement, hang it somewhere visible—on your desk, your classroom wall, or even in your planner. Every time you read it, you'll be reminded of your commitment to your students and the impact you want to make.

5. Mindful Reflection: The Power of Silence

In the hustle and bustle of the school day, we often forget the power of silence. It's time to carve out a few minutes each day for mindful reflection. Find a quiet spot, whether in your classroom, on a park bench, or even in your car (as long as you're not in traffic!). Close your eyes, take a few deep breaths, and let your thoughts flow while you reflect on a few key questions.

What do you love about teaching? What challenges have you faced? How do those challenges connect to your initial "why"? Allow yourself to feel whatever comes up without judgment. Sometimes all you need is a little stillness to hear the whispers of your passion calling you back.

To deepen this practice, keep a journal specifically for your reflections. Write down your thoughts after each session. You might be surprised by the clarity that emerges from just a few moments of quiet.

6. Create an Inspiration Playlist

Music has an incredible ability to uplift our spirits and inspire us to take action. So why not create an inspiration playlist filled with songs that remind you of your "why"? Choose tracks that resonate with your teaching journey—songs that make you feel empowered, motivated, and ready to conquer the world.

When you're feeling overwhelmed or disconnected, play that playlist in the background while you plan lessons or grade papers. Let the music wash over you and reignite that passion for teaching. You might even find yourself dancing a little in your chair. Don't fight it—let it happen!

7. Connect with Your Students' Stories

One of the most powerful ways to reconnect with your purpose is to immerse yourself in your students' lives. Make a point to learn about their stories, interests, and dreams. This can be as simple as having a conversation during lunch or conducting a "Getting to Know You" activity at the beginning of the year.

One of my favorite ways to connect with students is a simple ritual I call "Weekend Update." Every Monday, before we crack open a textbook or dive into any activity, I give each student thirty seconds to share a highlight from their weekend. Academically, it sharpens their ability to summarize and speak concisely—but honestly it's so much more than that. I learn things I never would've known otherwise. Like the student who proudly shared she was preparing for her bat mitzvah photo shoot or the boys who lit up talking about their soccer tournament wins. And how could I forget the quiet student who casually mentioned she won first place in an Irish folk dance competition, prompting an impromptu demo that left the whole class clapping. I also join in and share something from my own weekend, whether it's a concert I went to or a new recipe I tried. These little moments remind everyone that we all have lives that exist outside of school.

When you understand your students better, it becomes easier to connect your lessons to their lives. You'll find joy in teaching when you see how your lessons make a difference in their understanding and growth. Plus building those relationships can reignite your passion and remind you of the incredible privilege it is to be a teacher.

8. Join or Form a Teacher Support Group

Let's face it—teaching can be isolating, and sometimes you just need a crew who gets it. Joining or forming a teacher support group can provide a space for sharing experiences, challenges, and successes.

Organize regular meetups (virtual or in-person) where you can vent, celebrate wins, and discuss strategies for reconnecting with your purpose. These gatherings can serve as a reminder that you're not alone in your teaching journey. Hearing others share their "why" can inspire you to reflect on your own and even spark new ideas.

9. Take a Professional Development Break

We often think of professional development as something we *have* to do, but it can also be a chance to rediscover our passion. Look for workshops, conferences, or online courses that align with your interests. Choose topics that excite you—whether they involve incorporating art into your lessons, exploring innovative teaching methods, or diving into social-emotional learning.

By investing in your professional growth, you'll not only learn new strategies but also reignite your passion for teaching. Plus you might meet other like-minded educators who can inspire you.

10. The Power of Visualization

Visualization is a method many athletes use to assist them in reaching their goals. Ya know, they see themselves holding that championship ring or wearing that gold medal. But this method isn't just for athletes; it can work wonders for teachers too!

Take a moment to close your eyes and picture yourself in your ideal classroom environment. How do you feel? What are you teaching? How do your students respond?

Recently I practiced this visualization technique as I planned my new Maymester course. For those unfamiliar, Maymester is a unique, teacher-led mini-term that lets students explore learning outside the normal curriculum. Instead of traditional classes, teachers design engaging courses based on their passions and expertise—everything from thrifting and soccer to culinary arts and even global travel. It's an opportunity for students to dive into new interests, gain hands-on experiences, and discover learning in fun, creative ways.

For my course, I pictured a hands-on, immersive class about the history and future of our city. With this process, I picture us exploring movie studios, going on scavenger hunts along the Atlanta Beltline, and visiting local attractions that bring our lessons to life. I see myself invigorated, buzzing with excitement, and the kids feed off that energy. They're working collaboratively, asking thoughtful questions, laughing, and showing genuine curiosity. The classroom vibe—whether indoors or out—is filled with mutual respect and a shared sense of wonder. I then ask myself these questions: What habits, boundaries, or mind-set shifts would it take to make these thoughts a reality?

Visualizing your success and reconnecting with your "why" can help reinforce your commitment to your goals. You can even create a vision board to keep those images front and center. Cut out photos, quotes, and images that represent your teaching dreams and display them prominently.

Finding My "Why" During Difficult Times

Let's take a trip down memory lane. Picture this: It's the start of a new school year, and I'm feeling like a superhero ready to save the world—my classroom is decorated, my lessons are planned, and I've even made cute little name tags for my students. But as the weeks roll on, that superhero cape starts to feel more like a weighted blanket, and the enthusiasm I had for teaching begins to fade into a distant memory.

What happened, you ask? Life, that's what. I found myself grappling with personal challenges that seeped into my professional life. You know those moments when everything feels like it's spiraling out of control? That was my reality. It felt like I was living in a perpetual fog, going through the motions, but not really connecting with my students or my passion.

One particularly rough day, I remember sitting at my desk during lunch, staring at my uneaten sandwich while my students laughed and chatted in the background. It was a stark reminder that I was physically present but emotionally absent. That's when it hit me: I had to dig deep and remind myself why I chose to teach in the first place.

Fast-forward to a few weeks later, and I decided to take a leap of faith. I walked into the classroom with a renewed sense of purpose. I turned off the PowerPoints, pushed aside the textbooks, and simply talked to my students. We started a discussion about their lives, their dreams, and even their fears. I asked them to share something they were passionate about, and you know what? They opened up like flowers in the sunshine.

That day I heard stories of resilience, determination, and hope from students who, up to this point, I thought I barely knew. Their laughter, their seriousness, and their insights began to lift the fog that had clouded my mind. As they spoke I realized that these kids were why I had become a teacher in the first place—they were full of potential, dreams, and untapped creativity. My purpose came rushing back to me like a tidal wave, and I felt a warmth spread through my chest that had been missing for far too long.

Journaling Prompts to Reignite Your Passion for Teaching

All right, fam, let's talk about one of my favorite activities that can help you reconnect with your "why" in a deeply personal way: journaling. Seriously, don't roll your eyes just yet. Journaling doesn't have to be a tedious task filled with cringeworthy reflections. It can be a fun and enlightening journey of self-discovery. Plus it's a great way to unload all those swirling thoughts in your head while giving your soul a little TLC.

To help you spark that passion, I've put together some journaling prompts that will get your creative juices flowing. So grab your favorite pen, find a cozy spot (preferably not in the teachers' lounge during lunch), and let's dive in!

1. What Inspired You to Become a Teacher?

Take a moment to reflect on your initial motivations for becoming an educator. Was it a particular teacher who inspired you? Did you always love working with kids? Write down your earliest memories of wanting to teach. Try to remember the excitement and hope you felt—let it wash over you again.

2. What Are Your Favorite Moments in the Classroom?

Think about the times when everything just clicked. Maybe a student finally understood a tough concept, or you shared a laugh that made the classroom feel alive. Jot down those favorite moments. What did they teach you about why you love this profession?

3. Describe a Student Who Made a Lasting Impact on You.

Pick a student who stands out in your memory. What made them unique? How did they change your perspective as an educator? Reflecting on your students' impact can remind you of the importance of your role in their lives and reignite your passion.

4. What Challenges Have You Overcome, and What Did You Learn from Them?

Teaching isn't always sunshine and rainbows; sometimes it's a stormy mess. Write about a challenge you faced and describe how you navigated through it. What did you learn about yourself and your teaching style? Understanding your growth can be a powerful motivator to keep pushing forward.

5. If You Could Create the Perfect Lesson, What Would It Look Like?

Dream big! Envision a lesson that excites both you and your students. What subject would you teach? What activities would you incorporate? Imagine the materials, the atmosphere, and the engagement. Writing your dream plan out can remind you of the creativity that drew you to teaching in the first place.

6. How Do You Want to Be Remembered by Your Students?

Think about the legacy you want to leave behind. What do you hope your students take away from your classroom? Write down the qualities you want to embody as a teacher and the lessons you want to impart. This reflection can help clarify your purpose.

7. What Self-Care Practices Can You Implement to Recharge?

Teaching can be draining, and it's essential to prioritize self-care. List some activities that help you recharge and bring you joy. Whether it's going for a walk, reading, or enjoying a hobby, write down how you can incorporate these practices into your routine.

8. What New Skills or Strategies Would You Like to Explore?

Education is always evolving, and you should be too. What's something you've always wanted to learn? A new teaching strategy, a different subject area, or even a tech tool? Write about your aspirations and strategize how to explore them.

9. How Can You Foster Connections with Your Students?

Building relationships is the key to effective teaching. Reflect on ways you can deepen your connection with your students. What small gestures can you incorporate daily to show them you care? Brainstorm a few ideas and jot them down.

10. What Does Your Ideal Classroom Look Like?

Visualize your dream classroom. What colors are on the walls? What types of furniture are present? How do students interact in this space? Write about the atmosphere you want to create and how it reflects your teaching philosophy.

These prompts are just the beginning of your journey back to your passion for teaching. There's no right or wrong way to approach this—just write from the heart. Allow yourself the freedom to explore your thoughts and feelings. Remember, teaching is not just a job; it's a calling that requires love, patience, and self-reflection.

As you journal don't forget to celebrate your small victories. Each time you reconnect with your purpose, you're taking a step toward reigniting the passion that initially drew you to this beautiful profession. So get to writing and let your words guide you back to the heart of teaching. Your "why" is waiting, and it's time to embrace it with open arms.

The Takeaways

Reconnecting with your sense of purpose as a teacher isn't a one-time event; it's an ongoing journey. It requires intention, reflection, and sometimes a little bit of creativity. But the beauty of teaching is that it's never too late to reignite that passion.

Your "why" is the North Star when you're drowning in email chains about field trip permission slips. It's the anchor when the lesson you planned gets derailed by a fire drill *and* a kid accidentally spilling juice on your stack of graded essays. Maybe your "why" is seeing that lightbulb moment when a student finally gets it. Or it's knowing that you're shaping the next generation of dreamers, doers, and leaders. Whatever your reason, it's your steady reminder that what you do matters.

Remembering your "why" helps you stay focused when everything around you feels like a mess. It keeps you grounded, even when you're tempted to scream into the void (or into your coffee mug) during a particularly rough day. It's not about ignoring the challenges—it's about not letting the challenges define your experience. Your "why" is the fuel that keeps you going when burnout starts creeping in. Because let's be real: The system will drain you if you let it, but your purpose? That's what keeps you going, pushing forward, and showing up, even on the hard days.

Chapter 8

CULTIVATING JOY IN THE CLASSROOM

See, What Had Happened Was: They Gave Me a Classroom of Boys

I am a boy mom through and through, and I have always thought I had a special knack for teaching males. That was until I was given a middle school English class that felt like the teenage version of a boys' locker room. Picture thirteen boys, mostly athletes, with enough testosterone to fill a gym.

In the midst of this majority male classroom, two very shy girls, who were so quiet I thought they might vanish if someone sneezed too loudly, were also assigned to my class. Most of the boys weren't exactly thrilled to be learning grammar rules or writing essays, and the girls were pretty much invisible among the boisterous, macho guys.

I had to get creative to break down those gender barriers. Though it was a struggle for weeks, I was determined to turn our daily grind into a place where laughter, competition, and celebration worked like magic.

We started each day with a "life update." Since the boys played sports, discussions were all about who won last night's game, who scored the most points, or a little teasing about who rode the bench. It only took about five minutes, but it set the tone and connected us. For the next hour, we'd dive into English with games and competitions that made grammar way more interesting.

These boys loved any chance to compete, so I made our lessons a series of challenges. I started with simple "boys vs. girls" games, and I secretly met with the girls to encourage them to band together.

It didn't take long for the boys to notice that the girls were actually dominating them academically. Suddenly they weren't just "putting up with" English class. They wanted to beat the girls. The competition turned into a cycle of the boys and girls pushing each other to do better, with the girls' quiet confidence driving the boys to step up their game. And when someone got an answer right or managed to explain a grammar rule correctly, we celebrated it, complete with high fives, daps, and applause.

By the end of the year, the class average had climbed a whole letter grade, and the atmosphere was filled with smiles and a kind of camaraderie I hadn't seen before. Those shy girls created a bond, and the boys learned the value of celebrating each other's wins. I wasn't just teaching a classroom anymore—I was leading a team.

Now as much as I loved finding my groove with that English class of rowdy athletes and shy scholars, I'm not the only one who's tapped into this magic. I've met all types of teachers in schools all over the world, teaching various subjects, and educating diverse populations of students. And each of them has found surprising, joyful moments in their own classrooms. They've found unique ways to create laughter, spark competition, and foster a culture of celebration among their students, often in places you'd least expect.

In the next few pages, you're going to hear from a squad of educators who have danced through the chaos, cried in the car (because, same), and still managed to find joy in this wildly unpredictable profession.

These aren't just "aww, that's adorable" stories—they're real moments from real classrooms where joy showed up in jokes, unexpected compliments, and students finally getting that one concept after two weeks and five breakdowns. These teachers come from every corner of the profession—public, private, rural, urban, elementary to high school, all with different vibes.

What I hope you take from these stories is that joy doesn't discriminate. Whether you're running on fumes or caffeine, joy is possible. When your class size is pushing thirty, your Wi-Fi is acting up, and your admin wants three different data reports by Friday, joy is still available. The point isn't to copy anyone else's story; it's to find your own way back to that place where teaching fills your cup instead of just draining it. If one of these stories gives you that little head nod like, "Yep. I needed to hear that," then mission accomplished.

Now look, I could've just filled this book with my own pearls of wisdom. And trust, I've got a treasure chest of them. But I know teaching isn't one-size-fits-all. Your school might have therapy dogs and kombucha on tap, while someone else is buying their own paper and dodging flying pencils. We've all got different hurdles, different talents, and different kids looking up at us like, "So what are we learning today?" That's why I brought in these other voices. While I'm proud of my own journey, I'm even prouder to be part of a community that uplifts each other in real, raw, and sometimes hilarious ways.

Sometimes the only thing keeping us from a full-on meltdown is a group text with coworkers who get it. I've learned just as much from my fellow teachers as I have from personal development sessions, and I've had my whole mind-set shifted by a lunchroom convo or a late-night voice note. We're better when we share the wins, the flops, the awkward parent interactions, and the moments that make us laugh until we snort. These stories are proof that you're not doing this alone—and that joy isn't some mythical unicorn. It's real. It's here. And sometimes it just takes someone else's story to help you remember where to find it.

No Comprendo

Jan Beckwith (Year 21)

It was barely 8 a.m., and my sweet, chatty middle schoolers were already louder than a marching band. The noise was bouncing off the walls, and my nerves were fraying. I remember thinking about the advice I'd received from my veteran coworkers: "Don't smile until Christmas." Maybe if I had listened, dealing with my students would not have felt like a circus.

There I was, fractions on the board and classroom chaos swirling around me. The chatter was out of control. A full-blown symphony of fast-talking, high-energy kids. They weren't being bad, exactly. They were just . . . excited. About everything.

Now it is important to know that my classroom is like the United Nations. My students are from Colombia, Vietnam, China—you name it, we've got it. English is a second (or third!) language for most of them, so the room often hums with a mosaic of dialects. You'll hear Vietnamese murmured between desk partners, Mandarin shouted playfully across the room, and Spanish bubbling in the back corner:

"¡Dame el libro!"

"你做完了嗎?"

"Bạn ơi, tôi không hiểu."

It's a beautiful chaos—until it's time for everyone to listen as I teach.

I usually rely on my trusty translator app. I push a button, speak, and out comes a monotone voice spitting robotic phrases in a billion languages. But sometimes I get overconfident. I think I can handle it myself. And sometimes that blows up in my face.

The noise level starts climbing like everyone is auditioning for a decibel competition. I throw on my best "I mean business" face (even though my natural tone and demeanor give everything but serious).

I raise my voice and count down: "FIVE . . . FOUR . . . THREE . . . TWO . . . ONE!"

Magically the chatter dies down. Heads swivel. Eyes on me. Except for one boy. One sweet, confident, completely unaware boy. He's still going. Full-speed monologue, animated hand gestures, clearly telling his seatmate something very important

"WARNING!" I snap, with all the serious authority I can muster.

He freezes midsentence, looks me dead in the eye—big smile, proud posture—and shouts, "MORNING! GOOD MORNING"

I freeze and the rest of the class stares in silence. And then I bust out in laughter, evoking an eruption of giggles. Turns out he thought I said "morning," not "warning." His whole face lit up like he had just won the lottery.

All the tension and the frustration immediately disappeared. How could I stay mad when this kid thought I was offering him a cheerful greeting instead of a stern reprimand?

It was completely ridiculous, but it was perfect and pure. I eventually learned that "warning" in Spanish is "*aviso*." But the real lesson was this: In the small messes of life, you get a choice. You can fume, or you can laugh. So when I feel my patience running thin, I think of that little boy, I take a breath, and I remember that life's just better when you let yourself get lost in the joy.

The Sound of Music

Tasheina Canty-White (Year 16)

I am an elementary music teacher. I know you might be thinking my job is fluffy, but I guarantee you this job is not for the faint at heart. Right now I serve 840 students on a weekly basis. Yeah! That's 840 little spirits, personalities, behaviors, and learning styles. Now add allergies, behavior plans, and IEPs on top of that. While I absolutely love teaching music, there are many days when the beat of the music is about the only thing carrying me.

There was one particular day when I was teaching first grade. I was seated on a short stool and the students were seated right in front of me on the carpet. I believe I had just finished reading them a sound story. These are listening comprehension stories where students listen for their assigned cue word and play their instrument when the teacher reads it. As I finished my assessment via class discussion, I noticed a little hand go up. The kids were all engaged, and all eyes were on me. I acknowledged the curly blonde who'd raised her hand. I thought she had a question about the story. Instead she caught me completely off guard.

If you've ever spent time around young children, you know exactly what I'm talking about. This precious little first grader proceeded to ask me, "Ms. White, you like your job, don't you?" My eyes stretched while leaning back in shock. I replied with a simple, "Yes." She, along with three or four other girls near her all said, "We can tell!" The whole class then began to nod in agreement. Y'all, these were six-year-olds letting me know that they saw me and my intentions. They saw that my heart was in what I was teaching. My God, what a revelation! Comments began to ring out one by one: "We like music!" "We like coming to music!" "We like you!"

That one moment let me know that you cannot fool children. It also gave me unexpected joy! I used to think that I didn't need kids to like me as long as I was teaching them what they needed. These children gave me their stamp of approval. Not only did they say they like music, but they said they could tell I like it too! One of my favorite mentors, Rita Pierson, once said, "Kids can't learn from people they don't like." I now know this for myself.

That moment motivated me to never walk into my classroom with a half-done lesson or a negative attitude. If the six-year-olds can see it, imagine what the ten– and eleven-year-olds can interpret from how we teach them! As tired as I am some days, I ask God to renew me daily. I can literally drag myself into work, but as soon as first period hits, something on the inside wakes me up and reminds me to give my all and the children will see it.

In Your Face

Corliss Reese (Year 25)

My life as a teacher in a diverse middle–high school has its challenging times, and it has its times of sheer fun. Each and every day brings something new, especially with my younger students, who have a knack for asking the most interesting questions and finding the most unexpected ways to surprise me. With learners from so many different backgrounds, I work hard each day to make sure my lessons are engaging and meaningful. I'm always searching for ways to connect with my students and to give them that lightbulb moment that makes them remember a concept long after they've left my classroom.

One day I was teaching my fifth graders the difference between *implicit* and *explicit.* I wanted to be sure that it stuck, so I decided to be a little dramatic.

"All right, class," I said, pacing at the front of the room like a lawyer delivering a closing argument. "Let's talk about *implicit.* When something is implicit, it's implied, like a secret message hidden in a code." Then I started to tell them about the word *explicit.* "But *explicit*? Oh no, *explicit* is different. *Explicit* means it's in your face!"

To drive that point home, I clapped my hands loudly and sharply in the direction of the students. They all immediately burst out in laughter. A few kids began mimicking the clap and saying, "In your face!" while others repeated the words to themselves, testing out the gesture. It felt like a small victory. Seeing their reactions made me hope that they would keep that memory for some time to come.

Fast-forward a year, and one of my former fifth graders, Leah, was back in my class for a science lesson. This time around, I was teaching about ecosystems and explaining relationships between species. I casually said, "This is an explicit relationship. Do you all know what *explicit* means?"

Before I could even finish the question, Leah's eyes lit up and got big, and her hand shot into the air. She didn't wait to be called on. Instead she stood up, clapped her hands in my direction—just as I had done a year earlier—and exclaimed, "It means *in your face*!"

The entire class broke out in laughter, and so did I. I felt a mix of surprise, pride, and joy. Leah had not only remembered the term but also the exact gesture I'd used to teach it. In that moment I realized something powerful: The little things we do to engage students matter. That simple, dramatic clap had turned a one-off lesson into a memory that could be transferred into other areas of Leah's learning.

After truly understanding this, I've embraced every goofy gesture, exaggerated expression, and quirky demonstration I can think of. If a simple clap can make a concept unforgettable, who knows what a silly dance or a dramatic reenactment might do? Teaching isn't just about delivering content—it's about making it come to life.

Having the Right Teammate

Amber French (Year 20)

Teaching at a prestigious private elementary school was, in many ways, a dream. The students were curious, the families deeply invested, and the campus felt more like a charming university than a grade school. I loved the freedom to create engaging lessons, the beautiful classroom spaces, and the school's commitment to whole-child learning. But as every educator knows, even in a great school, teaching is never easy. There were long nights of grading and the daily juggle of planning, prepping, and showing up with energy and heart.

What made the difference—what made it joyful—was having the right teammate.

Caryn Oxford was not only my teaching partner for ten years—she was my friend, my steady force, and my daily source of laughter. Together we navigated all the highs and lows that come with teaching and life itself. When the pandemic hit and remote teaching turned our world upside down, Caryn and I leaned into each other more than ever. We became accidental tech experts overnight, building online classrooms that somehow still felt warm, welcoming, and joyful.

If you walked by our shared classroom during those years, you'd still hear us laughing—sometimes at ourselves, sometimes at the chaos, and often just because we needed to. That laughter was contagious, and our students caught it. They felt the bond between us and knew they were safe, seen, and part of something special. We called it Team French—our family away from home.

Caryn made the day-to-day demands of teaching feel lighter. She intentionally took things off my plate, always saying, "You're such a wonderful, but very busy, mother—I just want to help you be even better." And for ten years straight, she did exactly that. Her selflessness, her sense of humor, and her fierce loyalty made every day better—for me, for our students, and for the school community.

Caryn passed away in December of 2023, but her presence remains with me. She is in the lessons we taught, the traditions we started, and the joy we created together. She lives forever in my heart.

Taken together, these stories reveal that joy often lives in the in-between moments. The first story of finding laughter within a language barrier reminds us that connection doesn't always require perfect understanding. It's about presence, patience, and a willingness to laugh at ourselves. That kind of moment could easily turn into frustration, but choosing to lean into levity instead creates a memory—not a meltdown. Joy, in this case, wasn't in the lesson plan on learning how to understand a specific language; it was in the shared humanity. It's a reminder that even when the curriculum is clunky or the communication is messy, our ability to make students feel seen and supported can still shine through.

The second story, where students affirm their teacher by saying, "We can tell you love your job," is the kind of goose bump moment that every educator holds close. It's proof that our energy is contagious, and that when we show up with authenticity, students notice. Joy doesn't have to mean a perfectly executed lesson or Pinterest-worthy classroom. Sometimes it just means loving what you do out loud and letting that be the fuel. Kids are incredibly perceptive. When they see a teacher who enjoys teaching, they often mirror that attitude right back. This story speaks to the way joy is both an internal feeling and an external force that creates a more vibrant, trusting classroom culture.

The teacher who realized a lesson truly stuck years later reminds us of the long game of joy in education. So much of our work happens in the unseen, with results that take months or even years to show up. But when they do? When a student brings up an activity from years ago like it was yesterday? That's joy. That's impact.

And finally, the story of having a great teaching partner—but losing them—reminds us of the deep human connections that can form in the workplace and how those relationships can transform our teaching experience. It teaches us that joy in education doesn't just come from lesson plans or student outcomes. It often comes from the camaraderie, laughter, and shared moments with colleagues who understand the highs and lows of the profession. It's a powerful reminder that while teaching is serious work, it doesn't always have to feel heavy. When we find people who lighten the load with us, we not only become better teachers but better humans. And maybe we should take this as a nudge to seek out and savor those joyful partnerships or to be that person for someone else.

These stories, taken as a whole, tell us that joy in teaching isn't just about having fun in the moment (though that helps). It's about presence, connection, and the lasting imprint we leave behind. Whether through laughter, affirmation, or lasting lessons, joy reveals itself in many forms—and often when we least expect it.

Putting the Fun Back into the Classroom

There's a deep-seated belief that school is all about strict structure, sitting down, paying attention, and meeting benchmarks. But when you walk into a joyful classroom, that vibe shifts completely. It's a place where laughter breaks out at unexpected moments, where kids feel free to try new things, and where you can see the spark of excitement when they actually "get" something. A joyful classroom doesn't mean chaos, but it does mean you're embracing the little things that make learning enjoyable and memorable. And trust me, those moments are gold.

Firstly start looking for and intentionally creating moments of delight. Think about your day-to-day as a teacher. There's so much routine: attendance, handing out worksheets, collecting homework, checking planners. But in between those mundane steps are countless chances to break the mold and do something small that can make both you and your students smile.

For example, a quick game of two truths and a fib on Monday mornings can help ease everyone into the week. You might be surprised to find out that Alex really did meet a celebrity last summer or that Sofia has a pet iguana. Or, if you're feeling particularly bold, play telephone during a language arts lesson and watch the hilarity unfold as students try to pass a complex sentence down the line.

These little games don't have to eat up half the class time. They're quick, spontaneous ways to lighten the mood, give students a reason to giggle, and make the classroom feel like a place they actually want to be. It's amazing how a little laughter can set the tone for the entire day.

Sample Games for All Ages

Whether you're teaching elementary kiddos or high schoolers with serious "I'm too cool for this" attitudes, there are ways to integrate fun into lessons. I've rounded up a few ideas that can work for various ages. You can adapt them to whatever subject you teach.

Elementary School Games

1. **Fill-in-the-Blank Story**: Write a funny fill-in-the-blank story on the board or digitally, leaving out adjectives, verbs, and nouns. Have students call out suggestions to create a silly story they can read aloud together. This reinforces parts of speech with an extra layer of creativity.
2. **Number Relay**: Write math problems on index cards. Divide students into teams and have them race to solve problems for points. Award points for accuracy and speed.
3. **Shape Scavenger Hunt**: Call out a shape or geometry term and direct students to search the room for objects matching it. Just be sure to review rules of how you want students to identify the object.

Middle School Games

1. **Vocabulary Pyramid:** Think about the game show *$100,000 Pyramid*—but make it academic. In the original version, one person gives clues while their partner tries to guess the correct word or phrase that fits into a given category, racing against the clock. Instead of random pop culture topics or phrases, use current vocabulary words from your lesson on each level of the pyramid. Have students give clues to the person in the "hot seat" to see if they can guess the correct vocabulary

word. It sneakily reviews content while being fast-paced and high-energy.

2. **Graph It Fast:** Give students coordinates and have them quickly plot them on a graph. The first student to create the correct shape wins.
3. **Sentence Surgeon:** Write grammatically incorrect sentences on the board and let students "perform surgery" by rewriting them correctly. Each correctly "healed" sentence earns their team a point.

High School Games

1. **Debate Club:** Pick a topic related to the current social studies lesson, like a controversial historical event such as the Industrial Revolution or Civil War. Split the class into "for" and "against" teams. Allow students to articulate ideas and require that they use evidence to support their side.
2. **Protagonist/Antagonist Court:** Stage a mock trial where "defendants" are the characters from a story you've read in class. Students act as "lawyers," arguing for or against the "accused" character. This game combines drama with some literature and keeps students entertained.
3. **Scavenger Hunt Research:** Break students into small groups and give them a list of questions to research on the current lesson topic. The first team to finish with accurate answers wins. It's like a research relay race and keeps students engaged.

Incorporating games into your class is a way to embrace spontaneity. As much as we all want that perfectly orchestrated lesson plan, life just doesn't work like that. Humor, creativity, and flexibility are what make your classroom memorable—and joyful. You might not think of yourself as a comedian, but a well-placed joke or a touch of age-appropriate verbal irony (aka sarcasm) goes a long way.

And let's talk about creativity. Not every lesson has to stick to the book. Want to explain a science concept? Go outside and find examples in nature. Trying to teach about ancient civilizations? Bring in a "mystery artifact" for your students to analyze and guess its purpose. The goal is to find ways to keep them engaged and, ideally, make them feel like they're part of the learning process, not just passengers in the back seat.

Finally, *flexibility*—embrace it. Sometimes you might go into class with a solid plan, but if the kids aren't feeling it or you hit a topic that sparks a ton of questions, go with the flow. Let them lead the discussion or explore an unexpected tangent. These moments might not always feel "productive" by traditional standards, but they're often the moments students remember most.

The Takeaways

A joyful classroom isn't about forcing fun or sidetracking every lesson. It's about weaving joy into the fabric of what you do every day. Here are a few pointers to keep that joy alive:

Look for Laughter

- Don't be afraid to laugh with your students, or even at yourself sometimes. It's okay to be human in front of them.

Celebrate Small Wins

- Did someone finally master long division? Did another student give a fantastic answer in a class discussion? Celebrate it! These little acknowledgments help them (and you) stay motivated.

Give Students Agency

- Let students lead a segment, choose a class activity, or vote on the next read-aloud book. When they feel like their choices matter, they'll be more invested.

Take Mini Mental Breaks

- No one can stay focused 100 percent of the time, so add in a quick activity like a brainteaser or a short game to shake things up. Your students will be more alert, and you'll feel more in sync with them.

Creating a joyful learning environment doesn't require magic, but it does require heart. Joyful teaching is about keeping your enthusiasm alive and sharing it with your students, even when you're in your fourth week of state-test prep and everyone's dragging. Bring in humor, throw in creativity, and stay flexible—you'll find that your students will respond with just as much energy as you give them.

Chapter 9

TEACHING FROM A PLACE OF BALANCE AND FULFILLMENT

See, What Had Happened Was: I Realized the Power of Overflow

It was a regular Monday. I kicked off the "Weekend Update" with my class as I typically do. You know the drill: "How was your weekend? Do anything fun?" Most of my students gave the usual updates about sports and sleepovers while some responded with, "Uh, it was mid."

Then I got to Haley. She's one of those students you can't help but love. She's witty, sharp, and always laser-focused during lessons. She even had a smile on her face that day, but something about it felt . . . off.

When I asked how she was, she shared that she had a horrible weekend because of a family situation. I tried to lift her spirits with something generic like, "I'm sorry to hear that. Hopefully today can be a fresh start." That's when she responded, "It's going to affect my family forever."

I taught the lesson like normal, and Haley participated as usual. I later checked in with her privately. That's when she opened up about the news of her parents' divorce. We sat there holding back tears and sharing a quiet moment of heartbreak together. Finals week was in full swing, but here she was, trying to navigate life-altering news while juggling everything else. It was heavy.

Haley was navigating one of the hardest seasons of her young life, and the emotional toll followed her into the classroom. I knew immediately that this wasn't a situation where treating her "just like everyone else" would help. This was a moment for equity, not equality. *Equality* would mean expecting Haley to participate at the same level, on the same schedule, as her peers.

Equity meant recognizing that she needed something different. So I gave her space—space to speak if she wanted, or to stay silent if that's what the day called for. On tough mornings I let her step out for a breather without question and work solo during group activities. I didn't lower expectations out of pity—I adjusted the environment to give her what she actually needed.

I also reminded Haley that our school counselors were there for exactly this kind of support. I let her know she could go whenever she needed. She never took me up on it, but I could tell she felt seen and supported just by having the option. This wasn't about acting out of pity; it was about honoring her full humanity.

In that moment I realized something profound: My ability to support Haley relied on my ability to be present. If I had been consumed by my own stress, I would've missed the subtle signs, brushed off her words, and rushed through the day. But because I've worked hard to find balance in my own life, I could be there for her—not just as her teacher, but as a human who cares. I had been filling my cup and now had overflow, and that overflow could be used to be a better teacher.

How Balanced Living Makes You a Better Teacher

Here's the thing about balanced living: It actually makes you a *better* teacher. When you're rested, happy, and fulfilled, you're not just surviving the day. You're thriving, and your students can feel that energy.

When I walk in on Monday morning after a restful weekend, I feel like a new person and my students can see it too. I want my students to see someone who is fully present, genuinely joyful, and unapologetically human. I strive to present myself as both structured and approachable—someone who holds high expectations but also knows when to laugh, pivot, or just listen. Ultimately I want them to feel safe, seen, and inspired by the way I show up every day. Instead of dragging through Mondays with caffeine as my only lifeline, I am fully present. I am laughing along with my students and engaging with their questions. I am more patient, more understanding, and more fun.

When I'm living a balanced life, I'm not just a teacher checking boxes off from a curriculum. I'm a whole, present human who's also able to teach *whole* students. I notice their emotions, struggles, and quirks. I don't just hear their words, but I really notice what's going on with them.

Take Wesley, for instance. He usually flashes me a huge smile and follows it with the most sincere greeting and inquiry about my day. On one particular day when I greeted him, though, he simply said, "Good afternoon" with straight face. Because I wasn't rushing to pull up my slides or mentally replaying my own life drama, I actually noticed. Turns out he'd had a clash with another kid in a previous class, and I was able to nip that conflict in the bud before it escalated.

There was another time I could tell the whole vibe in the room was *off*. A quick check-in revealed my students were all exhausted from studying for a science test that they all mostly bombed. Knowing that, I could adjust my lesson, bring in a little encouragement, and get them back on track.

When I'm balanced I'm not stumbling through lessons or just surviving the week. I'm here—mentally, emotionally, fully—for my students. That's how I teach the whole child. It's not just about covering content. It's about creating a space where they feel seen, heard, and supported. And honestly? That's what good teaching is all about. It's not flashy. It's not about being perfect. It's about being present, thoughtful, and human in a way that lets your students feel safe enough to grow.

When you are teaching from a place of balance and fulfillment, you are not afraid to share a bit of yourself with your students. First decide what version of yourself you want to bring to the classroom. You gotta choose what feels true and sustainable. Then share selectively. Maybe it's a funny story, your favorite music, or a weekend win. Keep boundaries clear and when in doubt, ask yourself, "Would I be comfortable with this being replayed at a faculty meeting?" If yes, go ahead and share. If not, save it for brunch with friends. Connection doesn't come from being overly open; it comes from showing up and being real.

And if you're wondering whether balance and fulfillment really make a difference, don't just take my word for it—ask my students. They've seen it firsthand. They've felt the ripple effect of a teacher who sets boundaries, protects their peace, and shows up with intention. When I care for myself, I have more to give them. And they notice. Here are a few words from them:

- Blakely: "Your class is always fun and interesting, and I really like how you check on us to see if we're stressed with other classes. You actually change our due dates sometimes to help, but it's still hard enough that we learn stuff. I also like how you share little things about your life. It makes you feel real."
- Hannah: "You gave us a survey at the beginning of the year, and I can tell you actually read it. You started letting me work by myself more, which helps a lot, but you still encourage

me to talk in groups and speak up more. Thanks for always laughing with me and getting my weird little jokes."

- Aidan: "When someone is late to class, you have us give them a round of applause, so they still feel welcomed. Also, you incorporate our favorite songs and games into a lot of the lessons. I love that you always keep the class fun and energetic while also making sure that we are being productive and learning."
- Khady: "I have ADHD, and sometimes school is hard. But when you told the class you had ADHD and shared the strategies you use to cope, it made me feel better. You made it seem like it wasn't that big of a deal or anything to be ashamed of."
- Jayveer: "Although school can be a struggle, your class never fails to make me smile. Every day is a great day when I have your class."
- Shreeya: "When you found out I practiced Hinduism, you wanted to know all about it. That made me feel really proud. And when you came to my temple in a sari for Navratri, it was the best thing ever. That helped us bond and made me feel seen."
- Ricky: "You manage the class well and always find time to joke around with me. That's one of the best parts of class."
- Gabby: "You actually noticed when the girls were having bad hair days. I still can't believe you made a hair supply closet! I'll never forget opening that door and seeing hair spray, gel, mousse, edge control, combs, and brushes. You had everything—except a mirror! (We're using our iPads for now LOL). Thank you for bringing your extra hair stuff and helping us not feel like a hot mess."

Lessons of a Lifelong Learner

Balanced teaching means embracing the various roles we inhabit—even when they seem at odds with each other. Yes, we're teachers, but we're also learners, and there's a certain joy in seeing yourself evolve over the years. Teaching gives you endless chances to grow, not just as an educator, but also as a person.

For me, keeping my roles balanced has meant pushing myself to learn new things, like diving into mindfulness practices that I could then bring into the classroom, or attending workshops on social-emotional learning that transformed how I connect with my students. These kinds of experiences keep teaching fresh and they keep me passionate about what I do. But beyond that they give me a sense of purpose that goes deeper than lesson plans and gradebooks. Personal growth feels like an investment in myself—and, by extension, in my students.

Balancing my personal growth with my professional role hasn't always been smooth sailing, but teaching has also taught me resilience. There have been times when my responsibilities to my class felt like too much, times when I doubted if I could do it all. But those moments taught me to prioritize and to set boundaries that protect my time and energy. Growth isn't always easy, but it's worth it. And in the end, it makes me a stronger, more compassionate teacher.

And let me remind you, growth is a solo hike, not a race. Your journey to balance isn't supposed to look like anyone else's. So stop comparing your rhythm to that coworker who always has laminated everything by August 1. Instead, give yourself grace. Find a rhythm that suits your life. Maybe it's taking five deep breaths before you grade, maybe it's venting to your teacher bestie who *gets it*, or maybe it's finding a mentor who reminds you that you're already doing more than enough. You are allowed to evolve, stumble, and stretch all at once. That's what an authentic educator looks like.

As I have learned to embrace these various roles, one of the biggest lessons I've learned is how to embrace being an educator without letting it consume my identity. Yes, I'm a teacher—but I'm also a person with dreams, hobbies, friends, and a life outside of the classroom. For years I felt like I had to choose between the two, that if I was fully committed to teaching, I couldn't have a rich personal life. But that's just not true.

Learning to create that separation—learning to *shut down* on weekends, to leave work at work, to say "no" to things that don't serve me—was one of the most empowering decisions I ever made. It wasn't easy, but once I started living it, the benefits were obvious. I became happier, healthier, and more engaged in my own life. And paradoxically that's what made me a better teacher.

These days I walk into the classroom as my whole self, knowing that I am a teacher by day. I bring my experiences, my passions, and even my offbeat sense of humor. I'm not afraid to let my students see me as a person because I've realized that's part of what makes them connect with me. They see that I'm passionate about their learning, but they also see that I'm passionate about living a balanced, fulfilling life. And that, I believe, is a lesson as valuable as anything they'll find in a textbook.

But chile, I didn't arrive here overnight. Early in my career, I swung between extremes: trying to be the "cool teacher" or the overly buttoned-up version who stuck strictly to the lesson plan. Eventually I learned there's a space where you can be both professional and authentic. I didn't have to give students every detail of my life to make a connection. I could simply be present, warm, and consistent. That was enough.

If you're reading this and wondering how to start finding that balance for yourself, please know that balance doesn't equate to a spotless desk or a complete to-do list. Balance means you're carving out space for *you* in the busyness of your day. Start with one part of your life that's been whispering (or screaming) for attention. Is it your sleep schedule? Your social life? That half-finished art project you keep pretending isn't collecting dust? Choose one area and give it some TLC.

Little habits—ten-minute walks, Sunday night face masks, saying "no" without writing a novel of an excuse—go a long way.

Now let's get strategic about protecting your time, energy, and joy. Whether you're a first-year teacher still learning the ropes, a seasoned veteran juggling leadership duties, or somewhere in between, this is for you. Balance is not just a nice idea; it's essential for longevity and well-being in this profession.

Protect Your Planning Period

Your planning time is not a luxury—it's your professional right. It's not just for catching up; it's for getting ahead, breathing, organizing your thoughts, and setting yourself up for success. Don't give it away lightly. Yes, emergencies happen. Yes, a colleague may need a hand. But more often than not, if you're always giving it up, you'll end the day feeling defeated or depleted.

Try this:

- Close your classroom door and put a polite "Planning in Progress" sign on it.
- Don't be afraid to lock the door, turn off the lights, and work in a space where you are not visible from your door.
- If possible, leave your room to plan in the library or staff lounge—somewhere you're less likely to be interrupted.
- Silence nonurgent notifications.
- Let coworkers know that, unless it's urgent, your planning time is sacred to you.

Schedule Joy

We schedule the heavy stuff—meetings, trainings, observations—down to the minute.

Why not do the same for what fills us up? Joy isn't extra. It's fuel.

Block off time for something that brings you life. It could be twenty minutes of journaling before school starts, a midweek lunch with a friend, dinner with your boo thang, or a solo dance party with your puppy in the living room (we listen and we don't judge). The point is this: Put it in your calendar and don't cancel on yourself.

Ideas for scheduling joy:

- Add "Walk + Podcast" to your calendar.
- Set a recurring alarm for meditation.
- Treat solo lunch breaks or weekend matinees like sacred appointments.

One Boundary at a Time

You don't have to change your whole routine overnight. Start small. One evening a week, commit to a "No Work After Five" rule. Let your mind rest without grading, planning, or even thinking about school. Give yourself permission to clock out mentally and emotionally.

Start here:

- Choose one weeknight to be your "off night" and stick to it.
- Let your students, team, or even family know ahead of time.
- Use that time to recharge in whatever way makes sense for you—reading, cooking, a nap, a long shower, or just watching reality TV guilt-free.

Make "Me-Time" Non-Negotiable

Whatever your version of "me-time" is—gym, gardening, crafting, walking the dog, or doing nothing—it matters. It's not selfish, it's sustainable.

Make it real:

- Add it to your digital or paper planner and highlight it.

- Treat it like any other meeting: rescheduling is okay, canceling is not.
- Keep it simple. "Me-time" doesn't have to be glamorous—just intentional.

Swap Guilt for Grace

Stop waiting until you've "earned" rest by pushing yourself to exhaustion. You don't need to "deserve" downtime. You are already worthy of it simply by being human—especially a human in one of the most emotionally demanding jobs there is.

Let these reminders guide you:

- Rest is not a reward, it's a requirement.
- A burned-out teacher can't show up fully for anyone.
- Grace sounds like: "I didn't get it all done today—and that's okay."

The Takeaways

Teaching from a place of balance and fulfillment is a radical, necessary shift that changes everything about how you show up in the classroom. When you take care of yourself, you teach with overflow instead of depletion. The ability to notice, to pivot, to connect, and to teach with both structure and soul stems from how well you're caring for your own well-being. Here's what you should take with you:

Overflow Requires Intention

- When you're filled up—emotionally, mentally, and physically—you have the capacity to give to your students without draining yourself. Balance doesn't happen by accident; it is something you build on purpose.

Your Energy Sets the Tone

- A joyful, rested teacher creates a classroom environment that feels safe, engaging, and alive. Students can feel when you're fully present, and they show up differently because of it.

Personal Growth Fuels Professional Excellence

- Whether it's mindfulness, therapy, journaling, or buying a fan and learning the "Boots on the Ground" line dance, your growth outside the classroom matters just as much as your professional development hours. A fulfilled teacher brings passion and freshness into their work.

Boundaries Aren't Barriers, They're Bridges

- Protecting your time and peace allows you to bring your best self to your students. That means shutting the laptop at five, saying no without guilt, and treating your joy as nonnegotiable.

You don't have to be a martyr to be effective. In fact, the most impactful teachers are often the ones who've learned how to protect their peace while pouring into others. So if you've ever felt like balance is selfish or unrealistic, let this be your permission slip. Teaching from overflow is the goal. Start small. Start messy. Just start.

Conclusion

LIVING THE LIFE YOU DESERVE

See, What Had Happened Was: I Didn't Practice What I Preached

That night was supposed to be magic. I had it all planned: a glass of rosé, some warm bruschetta, and my laptop glowing like a beacon of creativity. I'd carved out this sacred time to write this very book you're holding. Writing it had become more than a goal; it was my therapy. After years of pouring into students, parents, and coworkers, this was my moment to pour into me. I was finally going to live out the dream I'd whispered to myself for years: Become a published author.

It was a Thursday, and I had designed a nightly writing rhythm that felt almost sacred. After school I'd go home, light my candles, put on lo-fi jazz, and type my heart out for two or more hours. That nightly routine was my reset button. But you already know where this is going.

I was halfway through my after-school pack-up ritual, ready to get the heck out of Dodge. The timer on my phone dinged—my sacred signal to shut down and reclaim my nonteacher life.

But no. Not today. Today my brain betrayed me with a soft whisper: "Just ten more minutes. You've got this killer Edgar Allan Poe idea. The kids are going to love it." Famous. Last. Words.

Ten minutes? Who was I kidding? That ten turned into thirty as I spiraled into full-on lesson planning mode, scrolling Pinterest for "Poe classroom activities," hunting through Canva for the perfect creepy raven clipart, and basically acting like I hadn't made a whole plan to put *me* first.

By the time I looked up, it was much later than I imagined. "No big deal," I thought. "I'll just run to the copy room to print the Poe booklets and worksheets I created on the way out. Quick exit. Easy."

Except—*plot twist*—the school counselor was still in the workroom. Sweet woman, really. But she had "some quick info" to share about a parent email. My internal dialogue was begging: "Girl, just forward me the email. Please." But something about her kind, worried eyes made me stay put. I couldn't bring myself to say "no." Boom—another fifteen minutes gone.

I finally made a break for it, heading down the hall like I was in a jailbreak movie, only to be intercepted by not one, but two coworkers. They were mid-debate about whether "Let It Snow" by Boyz II Men or Chris Brown's "This Christmas" was the superior holiday jam. And because apparently on this day, I lacked the ability to say, "Sorry, I gotta run," I weighed in. (Boyz II Men, obviously.) Another fifteen minutes evaporated.

When I finally reached my car, I was a full hour behind schedule, stuck in bumper-to-bumper traffic, my brain fried, my patience gone. But the universe wasn't done with me yet.

I got home, dropped my keys, kicked off my shoes, and went to retrieve my laptop . . . Gone. I had left it at school. The one thing I needed to keep my personal dream alive—my *writing*—was sitting on my desk next to that stack of creepy raven worksheets.

Instead of sipping wine and typing the next chapter of my book, I was hunched over my cell phone, pecking out words with my thumbs like a teenager in 2005.

And *that*, my friends, is how I sabotaged my "me-time"—by breaking my own routine, dismissing my boundaries, and putting everyone else's needs (and Poe's creepy raven) ahead of my own.

Lesson learned (again): Routines are sacred. If you don't protect them, chaos will gladly take their place.

So here we are at the end of this journey. If you've made it this far, I'm guessing something here struck a chord. Maybe it was a chapter about setting boundaries, or maybe the stories of reclaiming time for ourselves resonated. Quite possibly it was this last story that reminds us that making a commitment to living a balanced life will require continuous work.

Either way I hope you've found a bit of inspiration to start building that balanced, joyful life you absolutely deserve. Let me recap a few of the key lessons we've covered. Because if there's one thing I know about teaching, it's that a good review session never hurt anybody.

So where do you go from here? Well, let me be the first to say that you don't have to flip your life upside down tomorrow. Change doesn't have to be some dramatic leap; it can be a quiet decision to start valuing yourself in small, meaningful ways. Maybe it's setting a boundary, saying "no" to an extra duty, or reclaiming your weekends for yourself. Making work-life balance is about finding pockets of freedom where you can, one choice at a time.

Finding balance could also mean having that conversation you've been putting off. You know, the one where you ask for a prep period, request more planning time, or tell your boss that you really don't want to teach the honors courses every single year. Trust me, it's empowering.

And if they don't respond well? Well, maybe it's time to start exploring other options. There's no shame in that.

Remember teaching is a calling, but it doesn't have to consume you. You're allowed to have a life outside of the classroom—especially one that keeps you energized for the work you do with students, and one that gives you a sense of purpose beyond lesson plans and grading.

Achieving balance isn't about having it all figured out or reaching some mystical state of perfect harmony. Listen, I have unconsciously broken a few of my own rules (and regretted it). I forgave myself and worked not to make it a habit. Instead, balance is about the journey. It's about recognizing when things are out of alignment and taking steps to bring order into your life. It's about giving yourself permission to have a life filled with joy, with things that aren't measured in progress reports or test scores.

If there's one thing I've learned on this journey, it's that personal fulfillment and professional dedication aren't mutually exclusive. In fact, they complement each other. The more I've invested in myself, the better I've been able to invest in my students. The more balanced I am, the more I bring to my work. Teaching is not about choosing between a life or a career—it's about creating a life where the two can coexist.

So go ahead. Take that trip you've been dreaming of, spend time with the people who make you laugh, learn something new, or just take a day to do absolutely nothing if that's what your soul needs. Be loyal to yourself, to your own needs and dreams, and watch how that choice empowers you in every other area of your life—including teaching. Teaching is a part of your journey, but it's not the whole story. So go write the rest of it.

ACKNOWLEDGMENTS

I would like to express my deepest gratitude to all the people who made this book possible.

First and foremost, I give thanks to the Creator, for planting in me an innate love for the written word and a deep passion for teaching. Your guidance and grace have shaped not just this book but the path I've walked as an educator.

To Dave Burgess and Tara Martin, thank you for immediately believing in my work and encouraging me to share it with the world.

To Lindsey Alexander, whose sharp eye and gentle guidance strengthened every chapter—your support was invaluable.

A huge thank-you to my fellow educators—Jan Beckwith, Amber French, Corliss Reese, and Tasheina Canty-White—thank you for sharing your stories and wisdom. Your contributions didn't just add to this book; they made it richer, fuller, and way more real.

To my students—past, present, and future—you are the heartbeat of my profession. You have given me a lifetime of experiences, lessons, laughs, and inspiration that shaped this book and will continue to shape those to come.

To Kevin Lynch—your constant words of positivity, your unwavering belief in my talent, and your vision of me as an established author have fueled me more than you know.

And finally, to my mother, who always checks in with the classic, "You still writing, right?" Thank you for keeping me grounded and persistent.

ABOUT DR. YVETTE DIXON LEDFORD

PHOTO CREDIT: J. AMEZQUA

Dr. Yvette Dixon Ledford has been in the education game for twenty-four years, showing up at every level—from tiny humans in early childhood to full-grown adults—in both public and private schools. She's done the classroom grind, rocked the admin hat, and pretty much seen it all. Through it all, she cracked the code on how to teach *without* burning out—and now she's here to help other educators do the same.

With advanced degrees in early childhood education, reading, curriculum studies, and multicultural education (because receipts matter), Dr. Yvette Dixon Ledford blends research-backed strategies with real talk to help teachers protect their peace and reignite their passion. When she's not empowering educators, you can catch her traveling, connecting with new faces, or whipping up something delicious in her kitchen.

Book Dr. Yvette Dixon Ledford for your next event or workshop! Her signature talks include:

- Boundaries, Balance & Burnout: How to Thrive in Teaching Without Losing Yourself
- Work Smarter, Not Harder: Building Sustainable Teaching Habits That Last
- Reignite the Spark: Falling Back in Love with Teaching

Follow along on Instagram @dr.yvetteledford for educator inspiration, wellness tips, and upcoming events!

MORE FROM Dave Burgess Consulting, Inc.

Since 2012, DBCI has published books that inspire and equip educators to be their best. For more information on our titles or to purchase bulk orders for your school, district, or book study, visit DaveBurgessConsulting.com/DBCIbooks.

The *Like a PIRATE*™ Series

Teach Like a PIRATE by Dave Burgess

Balance Like a PIRATE by Jessica Cabeen, Jessica Johnson, and Sarah Johnson

eXPlore Like a PIRATE by Michael Matera

Learn Like a PIRATE by Paul Solarz

Plan Like a PIRATE by Dawn M. Harris

Play Like a PIRATE by Quinn Rollins

Run Like a PIRATE by Adam Welcome

Tech Like a PIRATE by Matt Miller

The *Lead Like a PIRATE*™ Series

Lead Like a PIRATE by Shelley Burgess and Beth Houf

Lead Beyond Your Title by Nili Bartley

Lead with Appreciation by Amber Teamann and Melinda Miller

Lead with Collaboration by Allyson Apsey and Jessica Gomez

Lead with Culture by Jay Billy

Lead with Instructional Rounds by Vicki Wilson

Lead with Literacy by Mandy Ellis

She Leads by Dr. Rachael George and Majalise W. Tolan

The EduProtocol® Field Guide Series

Deploying EduProtocols by Kim Voge, with Jon Corippo and Marlena Hebern

Designing EduProtocols by Mark Wallace, with Jon Corippo and Marlena Hebern

The EduProtocol Field Guide by Marlena Hebern and Jon Corippo

The EduProtocol Field Guide Book 2 by Marlena Hebern and Jon Corippo

The EduProtocol Field Guide Math Edition by Lisa Nowakowski and Jeremiah Ruesch

The EduProtocol Field Guide Primary Edition by Benjamin Cogswell and Jennifer Dean

The EduProtocol Field Guide Social Studies Edition by Dr. Scott M. Petri and Adam Moler

The EduProtocol Field Guide ELA Edition by Jacob Carr

Leadership & School Culture

Autopilot by Rich Czyz

Be 1% Better by Ron Clark

Be THAT Teacher by Dwayne Reed

Beyond the Surface of Restorative Practices by Marisol Rerucha

Change the Narrative by Henry J. Turner and Kathy Lopes

Choosing to See by Pamela Seda and Kyndall Brown

Culturize by Jimmy Casas

Discipline Win by Andy Jacks

Educate Me! by Dr. Shree Walker with Micheal D. Ison

Escaping the School Leader's Dunk Tank by Rebecca Coda and Rick Jetter

Fight Song by Kim Bearden

From Teacher to Leader by Starr Sackstein

If the Dance Floor Is Empty, Change the Song by Joe Clark

The Innovator's Mindset by George Couros

It's OK to Say "They" by Christy Whittlesey

Kids Deserve It! by Todd Nesloney and Adam Welcome

Leading the Whole Teacher by Allyson Apsey

Let Them Speak by Rebecca Coda and Rick Jetter

The Limitless School by Abe Hege and Adam Dovico

Live Your Excellence by Jimmy Casas

Next-Level Teaching by Jonathan Alsheimer

The Pepper Effect by Sean Gaillard

Principaled by Kate Barker, Kourtney Ferrua, and Rachael George

The Principled Principal by Jeffrey Zoul and Anthony McConnell

Relentless by Hamish Brewer

The Secret Solution by Todd Whitaker, Sam Miller, and Ryan Donlan

Start. Right. Now. by Todd Whitaker, Jeffrey Zoul, and Jimmy Casas

Stop. Right. Now. by Jimmy Casas and Jeffrey Zoul

Teach Your Class Off by CJ Reynolds

Teachers Deserve It by Rae Hughart and Adam Welcome

They Call Me "Mr. De" by Frank DeAngelis

Thrive through the Five by Jill M. Siler

Unmapped Potential by Julie Hasson and Missy Lennard

When Kids Lead by Todd Nesloney and Adam Dovico

Word Shift by Joy Kirr

Your School Rocks by Ryan McLane and Eric Lowe

Technology & Tools

50 Things to Go Further with Google Classroom by Alice Keeler and Libbi Miller

50 Things You Can Do with Google Classroom by Alice Keeler and Libbi Miller

50 Ways to Engage Students with Google Apps by Alice Keeler and Heather Lyon

140 Twitter Tips for Educators by Brad Currie, Billy Krakower, and Scott Rocco

AI Optimism by Becky Keene

Block Breaker by Brian Aspinall

Building Blocks for Tiny Techies by Jamila "Mia" Leonard

Code Breaker by Brian Aspinall

The Complete EdTech Coach by Katherine Goyette and Adam Juarez

Control Alt Achieve by Eric Curts

The Esports Education Playbook by Chris Aviles, Steve Isaacs, Christine Lion-Bailey, and Jesse Lubinsky

Google Apps for Littles by Christine Pinto and Alice Keeler

Master the Media by Julie Smith

Raising Digital Leaders by Jennifer Casa-Todd

Reality Bytes by Christine Lion-Bailey, Jesse Lubinsky, and Micah Shippee, PhD

Sail the 7 Cs with Microsoft Education by Becky Keene and Kathi Kersznowski

Shake Up Learning by Kasey Bell

Social LEADia by Jennifer Casa-Todd

Stepping Up to Google Classroom by Alice Keeler and Kimberly Mattina

Teaching Math with Google Apps by Alice Keeler and Diana Herrington

Teaching with Google Jamboard by Alice Keeler and Kimberly Mattina

Teachingland by Amanda Fox and Mary Ellen Weeks

Teaching Methods & Materials

All 4s and 5s by Andrew Sharos

Boredom Busters by Katie Powell

Building Strong Writers by Christina Schneider

The Classroom Chef by John Stevens and Matt Vaudrey

The Collaborative Classroom by Trevor Muir

Copyrighteous by Diana Gill

CREATE by Bethany J. Petty

Ditch That Homework by Matt Miller and Alice Keeler

Ditch That Textbook by Matt Miller

Don't Ditch That Tech by Matt Miller, Nate Ridgway, and Angelia Ridgway

EDrenaline Rush by John Meehan

Educated by Design by Michael Cohen, The Tech Rabbi

Empowered to Choose: A Practical Guide to Personalized Learning by Andrew Easton

Expedition Science by Becky Schnekser

Frustration Busters by Katie Powell

Fully Engaged by Michael Matera and John Meehan

Game On? Brain On! by Lindsay Portnoy, PhD

Guided Math AMPED by Reagan Tunstall

Happy & Resilient by Roni Habib

Innovating Play by Jessica LaBar-Twomy and Christine Pinto

Instant Relevance by Denis Sheeran

Instructional Coaching Connection by Nathan Lang-Raad

Keeping the Wonder by Jenna Copper, Ashley Bible, Abby Gross, and Staci Lamb

LAUNCH by John Spencer and A.J. Juliani

Learning in the Zone by Dr. Sonny Magana

Less Talk, More Action by Allyson Apsey and Emily Freeland

Lights, Cameras, TEACH! by Kevin J. Butler

Make Learning MAGICAL by Tisha Richmond

Pass the Baton by Kathryn Finch and Theresa Hoover

Playing with Purpose by MIchael Matera & John Meehan

Project-Based Learning Anywhere by Lori Elliott

Pure Genius by Don Wettrick

The Revolution by Darren Ellwein and Derek McCoy

The Science Box by Kim Adsit and Adam Peterson

Shift This! by Joy Kirr

Skyrocket Your Teacher Coaching by Michael Cary Sonbert

Spark Learning by Ramsey Musallam

Sparks in the Dark by Travis Crowder and Todd Nesloney

Table Talk Math by John Stevens

Teachables by Cheryl Abla and Lisa Maxfield

The Magical CTE Classroom by Tisha Richmond

Unpack Your Impact by Naomi O'Brien and LaNesha Tabb

The Wild Card by Hope and Wade King

Writefully Empowered by Jacob Chastain

The Writing on the Classroom Wall by Steve Wyborney

You Are Poetry by Mike Johnston

You'll Never Guess What I'm Saying by Naomi O'Brien

You'll Never Guess What I'm Thinking About by Naomi O'Brien

Inspiration, Professional Growth & Personal Development

Becoming the BISON by Kim Gameroz

Be REAL by Tara Martin

Be the One for Kids by Ryan Sheehy

The Coach ADVenture by Amy Illingworth

Creatively Productive by Lisa Johnson

The Ed Branding Book by Dr. Renae Bryant and Lynette White

Educational Eye Exam by Alicia Ray

The EduNinja Mindset by Jennifer Burdis

Empower Our Girls by Lynmara Colón and Adam Welcome

Finding Lifelines by Andrew Grieve and Andrew Sharos

The Four O'Clock Faculty by Rich Czyz

How Much Water Do We Have? by Pete and Kris Nunweiler

P Is for Pirate by Dave and Shelley Burgess

A Passion for Kindness by Tamara Letter

The Path to Serendipity by Allyson Apsey

PheMOMenal Teacher by Annick Rauch

Recipes for Resilience by Robert A. Martinez

Rogue Leader by Rich Czyz

Sanctuaries by Dan Tricarico

Saving Sycamore by Molly B. Hudgens

The Secret Sauce by Rich Czyz

Shattering the Perfect Teacher Myth by Aaron Hogan

Stories from Webb by Todd Nesloney

Talk to Me by Kim Bearden

Teach Better by Chad Ostrowski, Tiffany Ott, Rae Hughart, and Jeff Gargas

Teach Me, Teacher by Jacob Chastain

Teach, Play, Learn! by Adam Peterson

Teaching Is a Tattoo by Mike Johnston

The Teachers of Oz by Herbie Raad and Nathan Lang-Raad

Teaching the Ms. Abbott Way by Joyce Stephens Abbott

TeamMakers by Laura Robb and Evan Robb

Through the Lens of Serendipity by Allyson Apsey

Write Here and Now by Dan Tricarico

The Zen Teacher by Dan Tricarico

Children's Books

The Adventures of Little Mickey by Mickey Smith Jr.

Alpert by LaNesha Tabb

Alpert & Friends by LaNesha Tabb

Beyond Us by Aaron Polansky

Cannonball In by Tara Martin

Dolphins in Trees by Aaron Polansky

Dragon Smart by Tisha and Tommy Richmond

I Can Achieve Anything by MoNique Waters

I Want to Be a Lot by Ashley Savage

The Magic of Wonder by Jenna Copper, Ashley Bible, Abby Gross, and Staci Lamb

Micah's Big Question by Naomi O'Brien

The Princes of Serendip by Allyson Apsey

Ride with Emilio by Richard Nares

A Teacher's Top Secret Confidential by LaNesha Tabb

A Teacher's Top Secret: Mission Accomplished by LaNesha Tabb

The Wild Card Kids by Hope and Wade King

Zom-Be a Design Thinker by Amanda Fox

www.ingramcontent.com/pod-product-compliance
Lightning Source LLC
LaVergne TN
LVHW010659110826
845149LV00014B/3158

* 9 7 8 1 9 6 8 8 9 8 1 7 5 *